KT-433-809

WILLIAMS-SONOMA

Thanksgiving
ENTERTAINING

RECIPES

Lou Seibert Pappas

GENERAL EDITOR

Chuck Williams

PHOTOGRAPHY

Quentin Bacon

FOOD STYLING

George Dolese

STYLING

Sara Slavin

TEXT

Steve Siegelman

fP
FREE PRESS

NEW YORK · LONDON · TORONTO · SYDNEY

CONTENTS

CELEBRATING SIMPLE GIFTS

There is something uniquely American about the idea that, on the fourth Thursday of every November, an entire country sits down to share a national meal. No matter who we are or where we hail from, on this one day we are engaged in the same activity. We come together with family and friends to express, through words, laughter, and the pleasures of the table, how grateful we are to have one another.

Yet for all the enjoyment, the prospect of hosting a Thanksgiving celebration can be daunting. It is, after all, traditionally a big meal with many elements to manage, not to mention all the shopping, decorating, and cleaning. And the desire to create a "perfect Thanksgiving," like the family celebrations created by our parents and grandparents, only adds to the pressure.

In fact, it is helpful to focus less on perfection and more on simplicity. And the simple truth is this: If your meal is genuine and satisfying, you and your family and guests will have a memorable time. That is a perfect Thanksgiving. And it is the idea brought to life in this book.

In these pages, you will find everything you need to create five different celebrations, from the traditional to the casual. Each one includes not only easy, seasonal recipes, but also plenty of creative yet practicable ideas to help you bring a festive mood to your home and the table. You can follow the menus and work plans as described, or you can pick what you like from various chapters to create a menu and a style that work for you.

Thanksgiving entertaining is about bringing people together to share the season's wonderful food, the warmth of home, and the bonds of family and friendship. I hope this book will make it easier and more enjoyable for you to celebrate those simple gifts when you take a seat at your Thanksgiving table.

PLANNING A THANKSGIVING CELEBRATION

Whether you are having a crowd for dinner or hosting a few people over the long weekend, the secrets to Thanksgiving entertaining are organization and planning. The more you can do ahead, the more relaxed you will be when guests arrive, and your calm, happy mood will set the tone. In that spirit, here is a planning guide to help you bring together all the elements you need to turn a meal into a celebration.

A Reason to Give Thanks

Before you begin making lists and setting tasks, take a moment to think about the spirit of the holiday. The first Thanksgiving was a harvest feast to give thanks for nature's bounty. The more complex the world becomes and the more separated we find ourselves from family and friends, the more precious that simple idea becomes. When you host a Thanksgiving dinner, a day-after lunch, or a leisurely breakfast over the holiday weekend, what you are really doing is giving people a chance to connect with one another by participating in a centuries-old communal tradition: giving thanks together over a joyous meal.

It is that sense of tradition that turns a large family feast into a Thanksgiving celebration. But traditions don't have to be hundreds of years old. This year, why not start a few of your own? It might be anything from an unusual family recipe or a special way of setting the table to a quiet moment of contemplation, a song, or a game you play after the table is cleared. Tired of turkey? Try the ham on page 84.

No room for a formal table? Move the meal to the kitchen, or, if the weather cooperates, bring the indoors outside and create a "dining room" in the backyard. Keep the parts of Thanksgiving you like and set aside the rules you don't. Then let new traditions spring up from the unique realities of your life—the region where you live, the local ingredients that are in season, and, most important, the things you and your family value and like best.

Picking a Style

Begin with the guest list. The number of people you invite, who they are, and the mix of adults and children will help you decide on an entertaining style. Four to six weeks before the holiday, call or write friends and family, especially those coming from out of town, to confirm not only their attendance at Thanksgiving dinner, but also their plans throughout the weekend. Make a separate guest list for each meal you will be hosting over the weekend.

As a first step, make a planning checklist to help you stay organized from the beginning.

- Decide which meals you will be hosting
- Determine a guest list for each meal
- Choose an entertaining style (casual or formal)
- Set a time for serving the meal
- Pick a room for the meal
- Choose a serving style (buffet, family, or restaurant style)
- Pick a color palette
- Select, borrow, or rent tableware and serving ware
- Decide on the seating arrangement, table centerpiece, and other decorations
- Plan an achievable menu that fits all of the choices you have made

Next, think about the best place to serve each meal, keeping in mind what is realistic for your home and the number of guests. If you don't have a traditional dining room (and even if you do), you can set up a table anywhere—in the kitchen, in front of the fireplace, or, if you live in a warm climate, on the deck. Remember that the meal can also move from space to space, with drinks served, for example, outdoors or in the kitchen, dinner around the table, and dessert in the living room.

Casual Entertaining

A casual Thanksgiving, served buffet or family style, is especially practical when you are hosting a lot of children. It is also ideal for lunches and brunches during the holiday weekend. A casual style makes it easy for kids to come and go, eat and play, without disrupting the flow of the meal. Although "casual" means a comfortable and relaxing meal with simple, satisfying food, you will find that a few elegant touches, such as cloth napkins, seasonal table decorations, and special garnishes, are much-appreciated ways to create a celebratory spirit.

Formal Entertaining

A formal Thanksgiving dinner can be a truly memorable occasion, as long as you don't confuse formal with stiff. Comfort is still important, even amid elegant trappings. Dress the table with your best linens, flatware, and china, and have a seating plan and decorative place cards. The menu can follow suit, with sophisticated food and drinks. Set something fun—a little gift or a whimsical decoration—at kids' places to help them feel included. Or, you can set up a separate children's table, and serve the kids first so they can start eating right away, while the adults move through the meal at a slower, more enjoyable pace.

Planning a Thanksgiving Menu

Now that you have decided on the style of your Thanksgiving, you can begin planning the menu. Start with one of the menus in this book, adding or substituting favorite recipes of your own, or mix and match menus and ideas from the various chapters.

Choosing Recipes

Be realistic. Put together a menu that requires a minimum of last-minute preparation. If possible, give the recipes a try before the holiday to see how well they match your cooking skills and the realities of your kitchen. You may wish to build in shortcuts, including store-bought ingredients like a pie crust or tapenade.

Think seasonally. Visit your local farmers' market for inspiration. This is an easy way to see what regionally grown vegetables and fruits are at their seasonal best. Let these ingredients and fresh flavors shine through in simple preparations.

Add regional accents. Incorporate recipes and touches that reflect the area of the country you live in or your ancestral roots.

Ask for help. If all the cooking seems like too much to handle, ask one or more of your guests to bring a first course, side dish, or dessert. Offer to provide the recipe for whatever you assign.

Choosing Beverages

Once you have settled on a menu, visit a local wine store for advice on selecting wines. Allow one bottle for every two or three wine drinkers. There are no hard-and-fast rules about which wines are best for Thanksgiving. Reds and whites can go equally well with the many flavors of the meal, and it's a good idea to offer both so guests can enjoy a variety of combinations. Always include a few nonalcoholic beverage options, such as bottled still or sparkling water or iced tea, allowing one quart or liter for every two guests. Consider making a special seasonal drink, such as hot spiced cider to serve with appetizers, or cranberry lemonade to accompany a lunch.

Serving Styles

The next step is to assess your menu, guest list, and level of formality to determine whether to serve the meal buffet, family, or restaurant style. Whichever you choose, offering drinks and appetizers before the meal is a warm, welcoming way to start the Thanksgiving meal.

Buffet service is the tried-and-true approach for Thanksgiving because it works equally well for formal and casual entertaining and makes it easy to organize and serve large quantities of food. Guests make their way through the buffet line, helping themselves to as much of each dish as they want, and once you set out the food, all you have to do is replenish the platters as needed. For large groups, set up a separate buffet station for self-serve beverages, like wine and sparkling water.

Family-style service is well suited to less formal Thanksgiving meals and smaller groups. Choose platters that are small enough to be passed comfortably. Consider serving the turkey on two platters, with a selection of light and dark meat on each, instead of a single large platter, which can be cumbersome. It is helpful to have a sideboard or extra serving table for setting the platters when they are not being passed; this also makes it easier for you to refill platters and bowls as needed. Put bottles of wine and water directly on the table.

Restaurant-style service, in which dishes are individually plated in the kitchen or served by the host from the head of the table, is elegant but involves last-minute work. It is a good option for intimate groups, for simpler meals such as Thanksgiving weekend breakfasts, and for more refined sit-down celebrations.

Setting the Scene

Whether your celebration will be formal or casual, you need to plan in advance how to set up and decorate your space. Begin by choosing a color palette that looks good with your tableware and the room. That palette will help you create a centerpiece, place settings, and room decorations that will work together to set a festive mood. Stick with two or three colors and a few complementary textures, such as wood, pewter, and foliage. The key is restraint and simplicity. For inspiration, take your cue from the chapters in this book, each of which sets the scene with a straightforward, yet distinctive color choice.

TIPS FOR SERVING TURKEY

Here are some helpful tips for purchasing, serving, and storing turkey.

- When buying a turkey, plan on about 1 pound (500 g) per person for an 8- to 12-pound (4- to 6-kg) bird, or 3/4 pound (375 g) per person for a larger bird. Purchase a larger turkey if you want leftovers for the weekend.

- To garnish the turkey platter, have on hand fresh herb sprigs, such as sage, rosemary, and parsley, and colorful fall fruits, such as crab apples, cranberries, and pears.

- If the carved turkey meat on the platter looks dry, moisten it with a light sprinkle of hot turkey broth.

- Use leftover turkey in sandwiches, salads, and baked dishes during the weekend. Cooked turkey can be stored for up to 3 days in the refrigerator or up to 1 month in the freezer. To prevent cooked turkey from drying out in the freezer, freeze it in turkey stock.

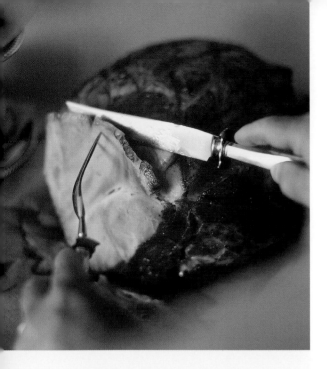

COOKING EQUIPMENT FOR THANKSGIVING

Well before the holiday, make sure you have the following equipment to avoid the need to improvise at the last minute.

- Roasting pan with large rack big enough to hold your turkey or ham
- Bulb baster
- Big spoon for defatting pan juices, or fat separator
- Sharpened carving knife
- Carving fork
- Instant-read thermometer
- Potato masher or ricer

Centerpiece

When planning your Thanksgiving meal, consider starting with the centerpiece, which establishes the look and feel for the entire table and provides a strong focal point for the setting. The centerpiece can be anything from a floral arrangement with autumnal blooms, to an heirloom bowl filled with seasonal fruits and vegetables, to a slender vase full of olive branches or fall berries on the stem. Pumpkins are lovely and colorful displayed on the Thanksgiving table. Keep the centerpiece natural and uncomplicated, and avoid too many tall elements that could block sight lines across the table. Use what is left over, such as branches and leaves, to make smaller arrangements for the buffet, coffee table, or mantel, or individual bouquets for each place setting.

Lighting

Dimming overhead lights and using candles or table lamps for illumination is an easy way to bring focus and sparkle to the table, even in the afternoon light. For an elegant setting, use tall tapers—dripless and scent free—set in candlesticks or candelabras. At Thanksgiving time, using silver, pewter, or crystal candleholders adds a formal touch to the setting. Classic ivory-colored candles go with virtually any setting and color palette. For a more casual gathering, line up votives in pretty glass containers or squat pillar candles along the center of the table or around the centerpiece for a glowing effect. Whatever kind of candles you choose for the table, add matching ones to the buffet to help tie the room together.

Seating

Don't worry if your chairs don't match. Thanksgiving is a perfect time to be creative with seating, and an eclectic assortment of chairs or even a rustic wooden bench lined with cushions can be inviting and attractive. To create a unified look, consider using colored ribbon to tie a sprig of leaves or berries to the back of each chair, or use single-color accent chair cushions. When making your seating plan, consider whether each guest will be comfortable in the chair he or she has been assigned and seat gregarious guests next to those who are more quiet to keep the conversation balanced. If your Thanksgiving celebration involves children, either seat them between adults or consider having a separate table for your younger guests.

Staying Organized

As your Thanksgiving plans take shape, it is important to keep track of all the logistical details and special touches that will bring the celebration together. This will ensure that you have enough time to plan as well as help you stay relaxed during preparations for the meal. Start planning earlier than you think you need to, and keep all your notes handy in a central place.

Make lists. Draw up a chronological plan that includes all of the meals you will be serving over the course of the holiday weekend. Go through the recipes you have selected and make a shopping list for each meal. Organize it by stores, including groceries, special produce, the turkey or ham, and wine and other drinks. Make a

separate list for decorative items, serving ware, and any kitchen equipment you may need. (Don't forget to account for any flowers, greenery, or seasonal items, such as gourds and pumpkins, you might want to use in your centerpiece.) Next, write out a schedule for each meal, working backward from the time you intend to serve the meal through all the preparations during the days leading up to it. Use the work plans in each chapter as a guide. Post the schedule and a menu for each meal in the kitchen, so you can easily refer to them as you work. As you complete each task, be sure to cross it off your list so you can chart your progress.

Plan ahead. The less you leave to chance, the more confident and relaxed you will feel when your guests arrive. Well before the holiday, take stock of your platters, bowls, linens, silverware, and tableware to see if there is anything you need to borrow or buy. Arrange empty platters on the buffet to map out how everything will fit; if planning to serve a meal family style, make sure your platters and serving bowls can both hold the right quantity of food and be comfortably passed at the table. If time permits, try out unfamiliar recipes ahead of time to work through any potential kinks. Stock up on staples like wine, bottled water, candles, and extra napkins. If you are hosting children, you might want to have some special games and books on hand in case they need a diversion. Buy some attractive take-out boxes at a restaurant-supply store to send guests home with leftovers.

A Thanksgiving to Remember

As with any kind of entertaining, the real work of Thanksgiving should be more in the planning and preparation than in the event itself. With a good plan in hand, you will be able to join the party and share in the fun. Once you have given some thought to the practical details leading up to the meal, use the menus and ideas in this book as creative inspiration. You will also find more practical information and tips about Thanksgiving entertaining starting on page 132. On this holiday, perhaps more than on any other, it is wise to keep things simple, abundant, and real. Cook what you love and serve your feast with joy, and you'll give your family and friends something to be truly thankful for: a celebration to remember.

PAIRING THANKSGIVING FOOD WITH WINE

TYPE OF FOOD	WINE MATCH
Appetizers and savory snacks	Sparkling wines *Champagne, Prosecco, California sparkling wine*
Turkey	Crisp whites or spicy, medium-bodied reds *Sauvignon Blanc, Zinfandel, Syrah, Pinot Noir*
Ham or other smoked foods	Fruity, medium-bodied white or red wines *Riesling, Gewürztraminer, Pinot Gris, Pinot Noir*
Roasted red meats	Full-bodied reds *Cabernet Sauvignon*
Rich foods such as creamed soups	Full-bodied white or red wines *Chardonnay, Merlot, Cabernet Sauvignon, Syrah*
Acidic foods such as salads	High-acid white or red wines *Sauvignon Blanc, Zinfandel, Chianti*
Desserts	Sweet wines that taste as sweet as the dish *Sauternes, Vin Santo, Muscat*

NEW ENGLAND THANKSGIVING

A sense of bounty and a menu featuring contemporary versions of classic favorites are the secrets to creating a traditional New England Thanksgiving that is both informal and festive. Have family and friends share in the cooking and bring a dish for the feast. To decorate the room, add a few well-placed touches of natural fall color. The warm wood of the dining table brings out the

old-fashioned beauty of cream-colored transferware dishes, vintage flatware, and crystal. Even if you mix and match china and serving platters, you can tie the table setting together with matching linen napkins, tucked with a spray of the same greenery used in the centerpiece.

MENU

Spiced Apple Cider with Clove Oranges

Roasted Spiced Walnuts

Baked Brie with Pistachios and Dried Fruit

—— • ——

Roast Turkey with Pan Gravy

Oyster and Mushroom Stuffing

Fresh Cranberry Relish

*Mashed Yukon Gold Potatoes with
Garlic and Chives*

*Mashed Butternut Squash with
Browned Butter and Sage*

Green Beans with Garlic

Rosemary Bread

—— • ——

Pumpkin Cheesecake

Apple and Cranberry Galette

WORK PLAN

UP TO TWO DAYS IN ADVANCE

Roast the walnuts

Make the cranberry relish

AT LEAST ONE DAY IN ADVANCE

Trim and blanch the green beans

Bake the galette and cheesecake

Bake the bread

THE DAY OF THE MEAL

Roast the turkey and prepare the gravy

Cook the stuffing

Prepare the butternut squash

Prepare the mashed potatoes

JUST BEFORE SERVING

Heat the apple cider

Bake the Brie

Sauté the green beans

TIPS FOR A CLASSIC THANKSGIVING

- Decorate the buffet with seasonal natural elements, such as pumpkins or other gourds, chosen to complement the colors of the table.

- Keep the place settings simple, allowing the wood tabletop—or a neutral tablecloth—to show through.

- Use the same foliage in the centerpiece and at each place setting to tie the color scheme together.

- Add accents of pewter—pitchers, salt and pepper cellars or shakers, and candlesticks—on the table and buffet.

- Present the bread on a rustic wooden cutting board.

- Serve food in a mix of transferware and traditional white or off-white platters and bowls.

PUMPKIN AND WILD BERRY CENTERPIECE

A pretty platter or family heirloom overflowing with autumnal branches makes a fitting Thanksgiving centerpiece. Choose an orange pumpkin and a small green squash that pick up the colors of the accompanying foliage. The less complicated your palette, the more focused your arrangement will be.

select a platter and gather the elements for the centerpiece: pumpkin, squash, acorn branches, and autumnal berries.

arrange the pumpkin and squash on the platter and tuck the branches beneath them, spacing them evenly around the rim.

fill out the arrangement with foliage and berries; keep it airy to allow elements of the platter to show through. Put the centerpiece in place, then scatter more sprigs of berries down the length of the table.

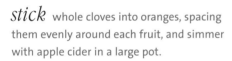 whole cloves into oranges, spacing them evenly around each fruit, and simmer with apple cider in a large pot.

gather mulling spices, such as cinnamon sticks and star anise pods. Wrap them loosely in cheesecloth (muslin). Secure the bundle with kitchen string and add it to the pot.

garnish each serving of cider with a cinnamon stick tied with an orange zest strip.

SPICED APPLE CIDER WITH CLOVE ORANGES

For a crowd of all ages, warm spicy cider imbued with fragrant citrus, cinnamon, cloves, and star anise is a welcome beverage at a Thanksgiving gathering on a chilly day. Keep the cider hot in a big pot on the stove or on a warmer in the serving area. Ladle into mugs or heatproof glass cups.

3 small oranges or tangerines, about
3/4 lb (375 g) total weight

36 whole cloves

3 qt (3 l) apple cider

4 cinnamon sticks, plus 10–12 sticks each
tied with an orange zest strip

2 star anise pods

Stud each orange with 12 cloves. Place the oranges in a large pot, pour in the cider, and set over low heat. Tie the 4 cinnamon sticks and the star anise in a cheesecloth (muslin) bundle and add it to the pot. Bring to a simmer and keep warm over low heat until serving.

To serve, ladle into cups and garnish each serving with a cinnamon stick tied with orange zest.

Serves 10–12

ROASTED SPICED WALNUTS

Both sweet and savory, these spicy walnuts make for crunchy nibbling to enjoy out of hand. This snack can be prepared well in advance and stored in an airtight container at room temperature. A slender rasp-style grater is the ideal tool for the orange zest.

Preheat the oven to 375°F (190°C). Line a rimmed baking sheet with aluminum foil and lightly butter the foil.

In a small bowl, combine the sugar, cinnamon, cardamom, cloves, salt, and pepper. In a medium bowl, whisk the egg white until frothy. Add the sugar mixture and whisk to blend. Whisk in the orange zest. Add the walnuts and stir until thoroughly coated. Spread the coated walnuts on the prepared pan in an even layer. Bake the nuts, stirring every 10 minutes to loosen them, until golden, about 30 minutes. Transfer to a bowl and let cool. Store in an airtight container for up to 3 weeks.

Serves 10–12

3 tablespoons sugar

2 teaspoons ground cinnamon

1/2 teaspoon ground cardamom

1/2 teaspoon ground cloves

1/4 teaspoon fine sea salt

1/4 teaspoon freshly ground pepper

1 large egg white

2 teaspoons grated orange zest

2 cups (8 oz/250 g) walnut halves

BAKED BRIE WITH PISTACHIOS AND DRIED FRUIT

Soft, warm Brie, jeweled with pistachio nuts and dried apricots and cranberries, is delicious spread on crackers or toasted baguette slices. The timing will vary depending on the ripeness of your cheese, so watch it carefully during the last few minutes of baking.

Preheat the oven to 350°F (180°C).

Place the cheese round on a rimmed baking sheet. Prick the top with a fork in a dozen places and drizzle with 1½ teaspoons of the liqueur. In a bowl, toss the remaining liqueur with the apricots, cranberries, and pistachios. Scatter the fruit mixture evenly over the top of the round. Bake until the cheese warms and softens, 8–10 minutes. Using a wide spatula, transfer the round to a plate lined with lettuce leaves. Serve with baguette slices and/or crackers.

Serves 10–12

1 round Brie cheese (1 lb/500 g)

2 tablespoons Curaçao, Cointreau, Cognac, or orange brandy

1/3 cup (2 oz/60 g) dried apricots, cut into 1/4-inch (6-mm) strips

3 tablespoons dried cranberries or golden raisins (sultanas)

3 tablespoons pistachios or pine nuts

Lettuce leaves for serving

Toasted thin baguette slices or crackers

ROAST TURKEY WITH PAN GRAVY

Use the neck and giblets to create a rich stock, then incorporate it with the drippings for a flavorful pan gravy.

1 turkey, 18–20 lb (9–10 kg), neck and giblets removed and reserved, brought to room temperature (1½ hours)

2 yellow onions, 1 left whole and stuck with 2 whole cloves, 1 quartered

2 fresh flat-leaf (Italian) parsley sprigs

¼ cup (⅓ oz/10 g) celery leaves

Salt and freshly ground pepper

Oyster and Mushroom Stuffing (page 33)

6 tablespoons (3 oz/90 g) unsalted butter, at room temperature

1 tablespoon minced lemon zest

2 carrots, unpeeled, cut into 1-inch (2.5-cm) pieces

¼ cup (1 oz/30 g) cornstarch (cornflour) stirred into ¼ cup (2 fl oz/60 ml) water

¼ cup (2 fl oz/60 ml) Cognac (optional)

In a saucepan over low heat, combine the turkey neck and giblets, the whole onion, parsley, celery leaves, and 8 cups (64 fl oz/2 l) water and bring to a simmer. Season with salt and pepper, cover, and simmer for 1 hour. Strain the stock through a fine-mesh sieve, discarding the solids. Cover and refrigerate until needed.

Meanwhile, position a rack in the lower third of the oven and preheat to 325°F (165°C). Rinse the turkey inside and out and pat dry with paper towels. Season inside and out with salt and pepper and loosely stuff the neck and body cavities with the stuffing. Truss the turkey or tie the legs with kitchen string. Place breast side up on a rack in a roasting pan. Spread 2 tablespoons of the butter over the breast. In a small pan over low heat, melt the remaining 4 tablespoons (2 oz/60 g) butter; stir in the lemon zest and ¼ cup (2 fl oz/60 ml) water.

Roast the turkey, basting with the butter mixture every 20 minutes, until pan drippings have accumulated, then baste with the drippings. After 1½ hours, add the quartered onion and carrots to the pan and continue to roast, basting every 30 minutes. If the breast begins to overbrown, cover loosely with aluminum foil. Roast until an instant-read thermometer inserted into the thickest part of the thigh away from the bone registers 175°F (80°C), 3½–4 hours total. Transfer the turkey to a cutting board, tent with foil, and let rest for 30 minutes before carving.

Meanwhile, skim off all but about 4 tablespoons (2 fl oz/60 ml) of the fat and juices in the pan, leaving the vegetables. Set the pan over medium heat and scrape up any browned bits. Add 2 cups (16 fl oz/500 ml) of the stock, stir over medium-high heat for 2 minutes, and then pour through a sieve set over a bowl, pressing on the solids. Use a large spoon to skim off the fat, then pour into a saucepan, add 4 cups (32 fl oz/1 l) of the stock (reserve remainder for another use), and simmer briskly over medium-high heat for 5 minutes. Add the cornstarch mixture and stir until thickened, about 3 minutes. Stir in the Cognac, if using, and simmer for 1 minute.

Pour the gravy into a warmed gravy boat. Snip the string, carve the turkey, and arrange on a warmed platter. Serve with the gravy. For turkey carving tips, turn to page 138.

Serves 10–12, with leftovers

OYSTER AND MUSHROOM STUFFING

Succulent oysters and woodsy mushrooms impart depth and richness to traditional bread stuffing. Bake any extra stuffing alongside the turkey for ease in serving. The topping will achieve a golden brown crispness.

In a large frying pan over medium heat, melt $1/2$ cup (4 oz/125 g) of the butter. Add the onions and celery and sauté until soft, about 10 minutes. Add the poultry seasoning and thyme. Season with salt and add the pepper. Transfer to a large bowl. In the same frying pan over medium heat, melt the remaining $1/4$ cup (2 oz/60 g) butter, add the mushrooms, and sauté until glazed, about 2 minutes. Transfer to the bowl holding the onion-celery mixture. Add the bread cubes, oysters, and parsley to the bowl. Drizzle with the oyster liquor and toss gently. Let cool completely before stuffing into the cavities of the turkey.

Transfer any extra stuffing to a lightly buttered baking dish, cover tightly with aluminum foil, and bake alongside the turkey for 30 minutes. Uncover and continue to bake until the stuffing is hot throughout and lightly browned and crisp on top, 20–30 minutes longer. Serve hot.

Serves 10–12

$3/4$ cup (6 oz/185 g) unsalted butter

2 large yellow onions, about 1 lb (500 g) total weight, finely chopped

2 cups (12 oz/375 g) finely chopped celery, including some leaves

1 tablespoon poultry seasoning

1 teaspoon dried thyme

Salt

$1/2$ teaspoon freshly ground pepper

$1/2$ lb (250 g) fresh small brown or white mushrooms, brushed clean and sliced

2 lb (1 kg) sliced firm white bread, cut into $1/2$-inch (12-mm) cubes with crust intact (about 8 cups)

24 oysters, shucked, or 1 pt (16 oz/500 g) shucked oysters, cut into bite-sized pieces

$1/2$ cup ($3/4$ oz/20 g) minced fresh flat leaf (Italian) parsley

$1/2$ cup (4 fl oz/125 ml) oyster liquor or reduced-sodium chicken broth

FRESH CRANBERRY RELISH

This tangy-sweet condiment is quick to assemble in a food processor. Both the orange and apple are left unpeeled for extra texture and flavor. Prepare the relish up to two days before serving so that the flavors mellow.

Quarter the unpeeled orange and remove any seeds. Cut the orange into 1-inch (2.5-cm) pieces. Quarter and core the unpeeled apple and cut it into 1-inch (2.5-cm) chunks. In a food processor, combine the orange, apple, cranberries, sugar, and ginger. Process until finely minced. Transfer to an airtight container, cover, and store in the refrigerator for up to 2 weeks.

Serves 10–12

1 large orange

1 large tart apple such as Granny Smith

3 cups (12 oz/375 g) fresh cranberries

$1/2$ cup (4 oz/125 g) sugar

2 thin slices peeled fresh ginger

MASHED YUKON GOLD POTATOES WITH GARLIC AND CHIVES

With their golden color and buttery flavor, Yukon gold potatoes are excellent mashed with a zesty addition of garlic and fresh chives. A quick sauté softens the heat of garlic to a gentle sweetness. You can make the mashed potatoes up to two hours in advance. Reheat them in the top pan of a double boiler over simmering water until hot.

5 lb (2.5 kg) large Yukon gold potatoes, peeled and cut into large chunks

Salt

6 tablespoons (3 oz/90 g) unsalted butter, at room temperature

12 large cloves garlic, minced

1½ cups (12 fl oz/375 ml) whole milk

½ cup (¾ oz/20 g) minced fresh chives

Freshly ground pepper

Put the potatoes in a large pot and add water to cover. Salt the water, bring to a boil over medium heat, and then reduce the heat to medium-low. Cover and simmer, stirring once or twice, until the potatoes are tender when pierced with a fork, about 30 minutes. Drain, reserving about ½ cup (4 fl oz/125 ml) of the cooking liquid.

While the potatoes are cooking, in a small saucepan over low heat, melt 2 tablespoons of the butter. Add the garlic and sauté just until it turns opaque, 1–2 minutes. Do not let it brown. Set aside.

Pour the milk into a small saucepan. Place over medium-low heat and gently bring to a simmer. Set aside and keep warm.

Return the potatoes to the pot and place over low heat. Mash thoroughly with a potato masher. Using a wooden spoon, gradually stir in ¾ cup (6 fl oz/180 ml) of the hot milk, the remaining 4 tablespoons (2 oz/60 g) butter, the sautéed garlic, and the chives. Add the remaining milk and, if necessary, the reserved cooking liquid, adding just enough for the desired consistency. Stir until light and fluffy. Do not overmix or the potatoes will turn gummy. Season to taste with salt and pepper. Serve hot.

Serves 10–12

Mashed Butternut Squash with Browned Butter and Sage

Golden butternut squash whips up nicely for this tasty and colorful side dish. You can make this dish several hours ahead; before serving, reheat it in the oven at 325°F (165°C) for 20 minutes.

Preheat the oven to 400°F (200°C). Lightly butter a rimmed baking sheet.

Place the squash halves, cut side down, on the prepared baking sheet. Bake until the squash is easily pierced with a fork, 40–50 minutes. Let cool slightly, then scoop out the flesh, discarding the peel, and transfer to a large bowl. Add the orange juice, half-and-half, nutmeg, and 2 tablespoons of the butter. Season to taste with salt and pepper. Mash with a potato masher or beat with an electric mixer until blended and smooth. Transfer to a warmed serving bowl.

Just before serving, in a small saucepan over medium-high heat, melt the remaining 4 tablespoons (2 oz/60 g) butter and cook until it turns golden brown, about 3 minutes. Drizzle the butter over the squash. Serve hot.

2 butternut squashes, about 4 lb (2 kg) total weight, halved lengthwise and seeded

1/2 cup (4 fl oz/125 ml) fresh orange juice

1/2 cup (4 fl oz/125 ml) half-and-half (half cream)

1/2 teaspoon freshly grated nutmeg

6 tablespoons (3 oz/90 g) unsalted butter

Salt and freshly ground pepper

Green Beans with Garlic

Trim the stem ends of the beans in advance and have the beans ready for quick cooking. You may also blanch the beans ahead and sauté them with the garlic just before serving. Parmesan curls add a nutty flavor.

Have ready a large bowl of ice water. Bring a large pot three-fourths full of water to a boil. Salt the water, add the green beans, and cook them until tender-crisp, 4–5 minutes. Drain the beans, transfer immediately to the ice water, and let cool for 1 minute. Drain again and pat dry.

In a large frying pan over medium heat, melt the butter. Add the garlic and cook, stirring, just until pale gold, 2–3 minutes. Add the beans and tarragon and toss to coat with the garlic butter. Season to taste with salt and pepper. Cover partially and cook, stirring occasionally, until the beans are heated through, 3–4 minutes. Top with Parmesan shavings just before serving. Serve hot.

Each recipe serves 10–12

Salt

2 lb (1 kg) small, slender green beans, stem ends trimmed

4 tablespoons (2 oz/60 g) unsalted butter

4 cloves garlic, minced

2 teaspoons minced fresh tarragon, or 1/2 teaspoon dried tarragon

Freshly ground pepper

3-oz (90-g) piece Parmesan or *grana padano* cheese, cut into shavings with a vegetable peeler (about 3/4 cup)

Rosemary Bread

Versatility characterizes this wholesome whole-wheat herb bread. It is excellent toasted, spread with fresh goat cheese and topped with sun-dried tomatoes, and served as an appetizer. Or, use it to accompany a cheese board at dinner or to build sandwiches for lunch the next day.

5 teaspoons (2 packages) active dry yeast

$2^{1}/2$ cups (20 fl oz/625 ml) warm water (105°–115°F/40°–46°C)

2 cups (10 oz/315 g) stone-ground whole-wheat (wholemeal) flour

About 3 cups (15 oz/470 g) unbleached all-purpose (plain) flour

$2^{1}/2$ teaspoons salt

3 tablespoons honey

7 tablespoons ($3^{1}/2$ fl oz/105 ml) olive oil, plus more for brushing

2 tablespoons minced fresh rosemary

6 cloves garlic, unpeeled

Sprinkle the yeast into $^{1}/2$ cup (4 fl oz/125 ml) of the warm water and let stand until bubbly, about 10 minutes.

In the bowl of a stand mixer fitted with the paddle attachment, or in a large bowl using a wooden spoon, combine the whole-wheat flour, $^{1}/2$ cup ($2^{1}/2$ oz/75 g) of the all-purpose flour, and the salt. Add the remaining 2 cups (16 fl oz/500 ml) warm water, the honey, and 3 tablespoons of the olive oil and mix on medium speed or by hand until well combined. Add the yeast mixture, 1 tablespoon of the rosemary, and as much of the remaining flour, $^{1}/2$ cup ($2^{1}/2$ oz/75 g) at a time and beating well after each addition, as needed to make a soft dough. Switch to the dough hook and knead for about 10 minutes. Or, transfer the dough to a lightly floured work surface and knead by hand for about 10 minutes. The dough should be smooth and elastic. Shape into a ball, place in a large oiled bowl, and turn the ball to coat the surface. Cover the bowl with plastic wrap and and let the dough rise in a warm place until doubled in size, about $1^{1}/2$ hours.

Meanwhile, preheat the oven to 375°F (190°C). Place the garlic cloves in a small baking dish and rub with $1^{1}/2$ teaspoons of the olive oil. Bake until soft, about 30 minutes. Peel and slice the garlic and transfer to a small bowl. Add the remaining 1 tablespoon rosemary and the remaining $3^{1}/2$ tablespoons olive oil and mix lightly.

Leave the oven set to 375°F (190°C). Lightly butter two 9-inch (23-cm) pie pans.

Punch down the risen dough and transfer to a lightly floured work surface. Divide the dough in half and shape each into a round, kneading out air bubbles. Place each round in a prepared pie pan. Use your finger to poke 6–8 holes around the outer edge of the top surface. Fill the holes with the garlic and herb mixture, dividing it evenly. Cover the rounds with a kitchen towel and let rise until doubled in size.

Brush the risen loaves with olive oil. Bake until golden brown and the loaves sound hollow when thumped, 35–40 minutes. Let cool on a wire rack.

Makes 2 loaves; serves 10–12

PUMPKIN CHEESECAKE

A gingersnap crumb crust underlies this spicy cheesecake, and caramel-coated pecans adorn the top, for an irresistible alternative to traditional pumpkin pie. Cut this rich dessert into small wedges to serve.

Preheat the oven to 350°F (180°C). Lightly butter a 9-inch (23-cm) springform pan.

To make the crust, in a food processor, combine the gingersnaps and pecans and process until crumbly. Add the brown sugar and melted butter and pulse for a few seconds to blend. Transfer the crumb mixture to the prepared springform pan. Use your fingers to pat the mixture into the bottom and evenly all the way up the sides of the pan. Refrigerate for 20 minutes.

To make the filling, in a small bowl, stir together the brown sugar, cinnamon, allspice, ginger, and cloves. In a large bowl, beat the cream cheese with an electric mixer on medium speed until smooth and creamy. Using a rubber spatula, occasionally scrape down the sides of the bowl. Gradually add the brown sugar mixture, beating until smooth. Beat in the eggs one at a time, beating well after each addition. Add the pumpkin purée, beating until smooth. Using the rubber spatula, scrape the batter into the chilled crust and smooth the top.

Bake the cheesecake until set or until a knife inserted into the center comes out clean, 35–40 minutes. Let cool completely on a wire rack. Cover and refrigerate until ready to serve.

To make the topping, set aside 10 pecan halves and coarsely chop the rest. In a small frying pan over medium-high heat, melt the butter. Add all of the pecans, sprinkle with the granulated sugar, and cook, stirring, until the sugar melts and the nuts are toasted and caramel coated. Transfer the nut mixture to a plate and let cool completely. Store in an airtight container. Just before serving, sprinkle the chopped pecans over the cheesecake and arrange the halves evenly around the perimeter.

Serves 10–12

GINGERSNAP CRUST

1/4 lb (125 g) gingersnaps, about 20 small cookies

1/3 cup (11/2 oz/45 g) pecan halves

1/4 cup (2 oz/60 g) firmly packed light brown sugar

4 tablespoons (2 oz/60 g) unsalted butter, melted

FILLING

3/4 cup (6 oz/185 g) firmly packed light brown sugar

1 teaspoon ground cinnamon

1/4 teaspoon ground allspice

1/4 teaspoon ground ginger

1/4 teaspoon ground cloves

1 lb (500 g) cream cheese, at room temperature

3 large eggs

1 cup (8 oz/250 g) pumpkin purée

TOPPING

1/2 cup (2 oz/60 g) pecan halves

1 tablespoon unsalted butter

2 tablespoons granulated sugar

PASTRY

1³/4 cups (9 oz/280 g) all-purpose
(plain) flour

6 tablespoons (2 oz/60 g) white
cornmeal

2 teaspoons sugar

³/4 teaspoon salt

³/4 cup (6 oz/185 g) cold unsalted
butter, cut into chunks

6 tablespoons (3 oz/90 g)
sour cream

¹/2 cup (4 fl oz/125 ml) ice water

FILLING

8 large Granny Smith apples, about
4 lb (2 kg) total weight

¹/2 cup (4 oz/125 g) sugar

3 tablespoons honey

3 tablespoons fresh lemon juice

¹/2 teaspoon ground cinnamon

1¹/2 cups (6 oz/185 g) fresh cranberries

2 tablespoons unsalted butter, cut into
thin slices

Sugar for dusting (optional)

APPLE AND CRANBERRY GALETTE

This beautiful open-faced pastry glistens with scarlet cranberries nestled among golden apple slices. Filled with already-simmered fruit, the galette bakes quickly and evenly.

To make the pastry, combine the flour, cornmeal, sugar, and salt in a food processor. Scatter the chunks of butter over the top and pulse for a few seconds until the butter pieces are the size of small peas. In a small bowl, whisk together the sour cream and ice water. Drizzle the mixture over the dough and pulse for a few seconds until the dough is smooth and clings together. Pat the dough into a ball, wrap in plastic wrap, and refrigerate for 20 minutes.

Meanwhile, to make the fruit filling, peel, core, and slice the apples. In a large frying pan over medium heat, combine the sugar, ¹/2 cup (4 fl oz/125 ml) water, honey, lemon juice, and cinnamon and heat, stirring, until the sugar dissolves. Stir in the apple slices and simmer until opaque, 5–7 minutes. Using a slotted spoon, transfer the apple slices to a bowl and let cool slightly. Add the cranberries to the juices in the frying pan and simmer until they start to pop, about 2 minutes. Transfer the cranberries to the bowl of apples. Boil the juices over medium-high heat until reduced slightly and spoon over the fruit.

Position 2 racks in the middle of the oven and preheat to 400°F (200°C). Have ready 2 ungreased baking sheets or pizza pans.

Divide the ball of chilled pastry dough in half. On a lightly floured work surface, roll out each half into a round about 12 inches (30 cm) in diameter. Fold each pastry round in half, transfer to the baking sheets, and unfold. Divide the fruit filling equally between the pastry rounds and spread it in an even layer, leaving a 1¹/2-inch (4-cm) border uncovered. Fold the border over the fruit, pleating the edges to form a broad rim. Lay thin slices of butter over the exposed fruit.

Bake the galettes, switching the pans between the racks and rotating them 180 degrees at the midway point, until the pastry is golden brown and the apples are tender, 35–40 minutes. Let cool completely on the pans on wire racks. Cover and store at room temperature until serving. Sprinkle with sugar, if desired.

Makes two 9-inch (23-cm) galettes; serves 10–12

CALIFORNIA THANKSGIVING

With its comfortable mix of informality and elegance, California-style entertaining can be a great way to give Thanksgiving a refreshing update. This menu has all the hallmarks of California cooking—fresh ingredients prepared with modern touches and Mediterranean accents that bring out the bright flavors and colors of the season. Carry that creative spirit through to the table

setting with simple white plates complemented with cheery pomegranate-red napkins and glass vases of olive branches. Offer the crostini and fruit sparklers as the guests arrive and mingle, then serve the meal family style.

MENU

Pear Sparklers

Crostini with Two Toppings

— • —

Butternut Squash Soup

— • —

Arugula, Fennel, and Orange Salad

— • —

Butterflied Turkey with Herb Glaze and
Chardonnay Gravy

Brussels Sprouts Sautéed with Herbs

Apple, Celery, and Sourdough Bread Stuffing

Wild Rice and Leek Pilaf

Anise Honey Wreath Loaves

— • —

Walnut-Praline Pumpkin Pie

Pear Tart Tatin with Brandied Cream

TIPS FOR A CASUAL THANKSGIVING

- Visit a local farmers' market and gather a selection of the season's most attractive fruits, such as persimmons, pears, and quinces. Arrange the fruits in low wooden or ceramic bowls or place them directly on the table.

- Use walnut shells as salt and pepper cellars, setting out a pair for every three or four guests.

- Line the bread basket with a patterned napkin or cloth that complements the color scheme of the table.

- For an intimate gathering, move the feast to the kitchen table.

- For a change of setting, serve dessert and coffee in the living room.

WORK PLAN

TWO DAYS IN ADVANCE

Mix the tapenade and goat cheese spread

Make the soup

Prepare the pie pastry

ONE DAY IN ADVANCE

Prepare and boil the Brussels sprouts

Ready the ingredients for the bread stuffing

Bake the bread

Bake the pumpkin pie and pear tart

THE DAY OF THE MEAL

Prepare the salad ingredients

Roast the turkey and prepare the gravy

JUST BEFORE SERVING

Bake the bread stuffing

Make the pilaf

Assemble the crostini platter

Mix the pear sparklers

Sauté the Brussels sprouts

Dress the salad

OLIVE SPRIG PLACE CARDS

Instead of place cards, use a sprig of olive branch, fresh woody herbs, or bundles of greenery that complement your centerpiece. Not only does it perfume the room, it's an easy way to soften and unify a contemporary table setting while bringing a touch of nature inside.

collect olive sprigs or fresh herbs, including some of the greens used in the centerpiece. Choose sturdy plants that won't wilt quickly, such as olive, sage, rosemary, and eucalyptus.

select a sprig or two, making one bunch or place marker for each dinner guest. Write guests' names on simple name tags.

tie the sprig or bundle with grosgrain ribbon or raffia, and adorn each with a name tag.

place a sprig on each napkin and arrange the tag at an attractive angle.

pour pear juice into tall, ice-filled glasses, taking care to pour directly into the center of the glass to keep the sides clean.

add chilled sparkling water to each glass, measuring the water for the first drink so that you can fill the remaining glasses by eye.

stir each drink with a long spoon until the liquids are completely mixed, and garnish with a thin slice of fresh pear.

Pear Sparklers

Upon arrival, offer your guests the option of this lively nonalcoholic beverage, a refreshing duet of pear juice and sparkling mineral water.

Ice cubes

1½–2 cups (12–16 fl oz/375–500 ml) bottled pear juice

4–5 cups (32–40 fl oz/1–1.25 l) sparkling mineral water

1 Anjou pear, for garnish

Place ice cubes in tall glasses. Add about 3 tablespoons pear juice to each glass, and then pour in about ½ cup (4 fl oz/125 ml) sparkling mineral water. Slice the pear into thin wedges to garnish each glass, then serve at once.

Serves 8–10

CROSTINI WITH TWO TOPPINGS

Crisp oven-baked baguette slices play the supporting role for two zesty spreads—one, a creamy goat cheese blended with fresh herbs, and the other, a lively tapenade of olives and sun-dried tomatoes. For a variation, you can omit the tomatoes and substitute 4 anchovy fillets, chopped.

To make the tapenade, preheat the oven to 350°F (180°C). Spread the walnuts on a rimmed baking sheet and bake until lightly toasted, about 10 minutes. Remove from the oven and pour onto a plate to cool.

In a food processor, combine the olives, sun-dried tomatoes, basil, toasted walnuts, garlic, vinegar, lemon zest, mustard, and cheese. Process until minced. Add the olive oil and process to blend. Season to taste with salt and pepper. Transfer to a serving bowl, cover, and refrigerate until serving. (The tapenade can be prepared up to 1 week in advance and stored, tightly covered, in the refrigerator.)

To make the goat cheese spread, in a small bowl, mix together the goat cheese, chives, parsley, dill, and garlic. Transfer to a serving bowl, cover, and refrigerate until serving (The cheese spread can be prepared up to 2 days in advance and stored, tightly covered, in the refrigerator.)

Preheat the oven to 325°F (165°C). Slice the baguette into slices ¼ inch (6 mm) thick and arrange on a rimmed baking sheet. Bake until lightly browned and crisp, 10-12 minutes. Remove from the oven and, if desired, brush with olive oil.

Serve the spreads atop toasted baguette slices, or serve the toasts alongside the 2 spreads and let guests serve themselves.

Serves 8–10

SUN-DRIED TOMATO AND OLIVE TAPENADE

¹/₂ cup (2 oz/60 g) walnuts

1¹/₄ cups (6 oz/185 g) pitted Kalamata or other brine-cured black olives

¹/₂ cup (2¹/₂ oz/75 g) drained, oil-packed sun-dried tomatoes, chopped

¹/₂ cup (¹/₂ oz/15 g) fresh basil leaves, or 2 green (spring) onions, chopped, and ¹/₄ cup (¹/₃ oz/10 g) minced parsley

2 large cloves garlic, minced

1 tablespoon balsamic vinegar

2 teaspoons minced lemon zest

1 teaspoon Dijon mustard

2 tablespoons grated Parmesan cheese

2 tablespoons olive oil

Salt and freshly ground pepper

HERBED GOAT CHEESE SPREAD

1 log fresh mild goat cheese, ¹/₂ lb (250 g), at room temperature

2 tablespoons minced fresh chives

2 tablespoons minced fresh flat-leaf (Italian) parsley

1 tablespoon minced fresh dill

1 clove garlic, minced

1 baguette

Olive oil for brushing (optional)

Butternut Squash Soup

3 tablespoons canola oil

2 tablespoons balsamic vinegar

2 butternut squashes, about 3 lb (1.5 kg) total weight, halved lengthwise and seeded

1 large Granny Smith apple or Anjou or Bosc pear, peeled, halved, and cored

2 yellow onions, quartered

6 cups (48 fl oz/1.5 l) chicken stock or reduced-sodium chicken broth

1/4 teaspoon freshly grated nutmeg

Salt and freshly ground pepper

1/2 cup (4 fl oz/125 ml) half-and-half (half cream) or 1/2 cup (4 oz/125 g) plain yogurt

1 tablespoon unsalted butter

1/4 cup (1/3 oz/10 g) chopped fresh sage

The subtle sweetness of apple or pear elevates this creamy squash soup. Roast the fruit and vegetables first to give them a caramelized taste. Plan to make the soup a day in advance to allow the flavors to mingle.

Preheat the oven to 450°F (230°C). Line a rimmed baking sheet with aluminum foil.

In a small bowl, stir together the oil and vinegar. Brush the cut sides of the squash, the apple halves, and the onions with the oil mixture. Place the squash and apple halves, cut side down, and the onions on the prepared baking sheet. Bake, turning the fruit and vegetables twice, until tender and lightly browned, about 30 minutes for the apple and 45–50 minutes for the vegetables. Transfer to a cutting board and let cool. Scoop out the flesh from the squash halves, discarding the peel. Coarsely chop the apple and onions.

Transfer the squash flesh, onions, and apple to a large saucepan and add the stock and nutmeg. Bring to a boil over medium-high heat and then reduce the heat to medium. Simmer until very tender, about 20 minutes. Remove from the heat and let cool. In a blender, purée the soup in batches until smooth. Return the soup to the pan, stir in the half-and-half, season to taste with salt and pepper, and heat through over medium heat. (The soup can be prepared up to 2 days in advance and stored, tightly covered, in the refrigerator.)

Just before serving, melt the butter in a small frying pan over medium heat. Add the sage and sauté until the butter browns lightly and the sage is crisp. Ladle the soup into warmed bowls and garnish with the sage butter.

Serves 8–10

ARUGULA, FENNEL, AND ORANGE SALAD

The bright flavors of peppery arugula, the anise accent of fennel, and the tangy sweetness of oranges come together in this vibrant winter salad. You can make the vinaigrette and prepare the fennel and oranges ahead of time and refrigerate. Combine all the elements just before serving.

To make the vinaigrette, in a small bowl, whisk together the orange juice, lemon juice, orange zest, olive oil, canola oil, mustard, tarragon, and shallot. Season to taste with salt and pepper. Set aside.

Cut off the stems and feathery fronds of the fennel bulb and remove any bruised or discolored outer layers. Cut the bulb in half lengthwise and cut out any tough core parts. Cut the bulb halves crosswise into slices ³/₈ inch (1 cm) thick, and then cut the slices into 1-inch (2.5-cm) lengths.

Working with 1 orange at a time, and using a sharp knife, cut a slice off both ends of the orange to reveal the flesh. Stand the orange upright on a cutting board and thickly slice off the peel and pith in strips, following the contour of the fruit. Cut the orange in half crosswise, place each half cut side down, and thinly slice vertically to create half-moons. Repeat with the remaining oranges.

Place the fennel and arugula in a large serving bowl, add half of the vinaigrette, and toss gently to coat thoroughly. Arrange the orange slices in a pinwheel or other design on top. Drizzle with the remaining vinaigrette and serve.

Serves 8–10

CITRUS VINAIGRETTE

¹/₄ cup (2 fl oz/60 ml) fresh orange juice

2 tablespoons fresh lemon juice

2 teaspoons grated orange zest

2 tablespoons extra-virgin olive oil

2 tablespoons canola oil

2 teaspoons Dijon mustard

¹/₂ teaspoon dried tarragon

1 shallot, chopped

Salt and freshly ground pepper

1 large fennel bulb

3 large navel oranges

4 cups (4 oz/125 g) arugula (rocket)

Butterflied Turkey with Herb Glaze and Chardonnay Gravy

A butterflied turkey makes a handsome presentation, especially when wreathed with rosemary sprigs and lemons. Fresh herbs and garlic, rubbed both under and over the skin, infuse the bird with flavor.

1 turkey, 12–14 lb (6–7 kg), neck and giblets removed and reserved

Salt and freshly ground pepper

6 cloves garlic, minced

1/4 cup (1 1/2 oz/45 g) minced shallots or green (spring) onions, including tender green tops

1/3 cup (1/2 oz/15 g) minced fresh flat-leaf (Italian) parsley, plus 2 sprigs for stock

3 tablespoons minced fresh oregano

3 tablespoons minced fresh rosemary, plus sprigs for garnish

3 tablespoons Dijon mustard

3 tablespoons fresh lemon juice

3 tablespoons extra-virgin olive oil

1 yellow onion, stuck with 2 whole cloves

1/4 cup (1/3 oz/10 g) celery leaves

1–2 tablespoons unsalted butter, melted

4 lemons, halved

Chardonnay Gravy (page 63)

Rinse the turkey inside and out and pat dry with paper towels. Position the bird breast side down on a cutting board. Using kitchen shears or a large knife, cut along one side of the backbone until the bird is split open. Pull open the halves of the bird. Cut down the other side of the backbone to free it, then cut between the rib plates and remove any small pieces of bone. Turn the bird breast side up, opening it as flat as possible, and cover with a sheet of plastic wrap. Using a rolling pin or your hands, press it firmly to break the breastbone and flatten the bird. Season the bird with salt and pepper.

In a bowl, mix together the garlic, shallots, minced parsley, oregano, minced rosemary, mustard, lemon juice, and olive oil. Use your fingers to push some of the herb mixture under the skin of the breast and legs. Rub the remaining herb mixture over the surface of the bird. Place on a baking sheet, cover loosely with plastic wrap, and refrigerate for 6–24 hours. Bring the turkey to room temperature (about 1 hour) before roasting.

Meanwhile, in a saucepan over low heat, combine 6 cups (48 fl oz/1.5 l) water; the turkey neck, heart, and gizzard (reserve the liver for another use); onion; parsley sprigs; and celery leaves and bring to a simmer. Cover and cook for 1 hour, then strain, cover, and refrigerate the stock until ready to make the gravy.

Preheat the oven to 375°F (190°C). Spray a roasting pan with nonstick cooking spray and place a rack in the pan. Place the turkey, breast side up, on the rack, and tuck the legs in tightly. Brush with the melted butter. Roast until the skin is crisp and deep brown and an instant-read thermometer inserted into the thickest part of the thigh away from the bone registers 175°F (80°C), 2 1/4–2 3/4 hours. Transfer the turkey to a warmed serving platter, tent with aluminum foil, and let rest for 20 minutes. Garnish the platter with the rosemary sprigs and lemon halves. Carve the turkey at the table and pass the gravy. For turkey carving tips, turn to page 138.

Serves 8–10, with leftovers

Chardonnay Gravy

This wine-infused gravy picks up the subtle herbal flavors—garlic, oregano, rosemary, and parsley—of the butterflied turkey and is an ideal accompaniment.

After transferring the turkey to a platter, set the roasting pan on the stove top over medium-high heat. Add the wine and heat, stirring to scrape up the browned bits on the pan bottom, until the wine is reduced by half, about 10 minutes. Add 4 cups (32 fl oz/1 l) of the stock (reserve any remaining stock for another use) and bring to a boil. Stir in the dissolved cornstarch and cook until thickened, about 5 minutes.

Pour into a warmed gravy boat and serve alongside the turkey.

Serves 8–10

1 cup (8 fl oz/250 ml) Chardonnay or other dry white wine

Reserved turkey stock (page 60)

1/4 cup (1 oz/30 g) cornstarch (cornflour) stirred into 1/4 cup (2 fl oz/60 ml) water

Brussels Sprouts Sautéed with Herbs

Fresh herbs give a fragrant lift to Brussels sprouts. The sprouts can be boiled a day in advance, chilled in ice water, drained, and refrigerated. Sauté with the herbs just before serving.

Cut a shallow X in the stem end of each Brussels sprout. Bring a large saucepan three-fourths full of water to a boil. Salt the water, add the Brussels sprouts, and cook until tender, 6–8 minutes. Drain thoroughly. Return the pan of sprouts to medium-high heat. Add the olive oil and heat, stirring to glaze the sprouts. Sprinkle with the chives and oregano and season with salt and pepper. Toss to coat well. Serve hot.

Serves 8–10

3 lb (1.5 kg) Brussels sprouts, stems trimmed and any brown outer leaves removed

Salt

1/4 cup (2 fl oz/60 ml) olive oil

1/4 cup (1/3 oz/10 g) minced fresh chives

2 tablespoons minced fresh oregano

Freshly ground pepper

APPLE, CELERY, AND SOURDOUGH BREAD STUFFING

1 loaf sourdough bread, 1 lb (500 g), cut into 1/2-inch (12-mm) cubes with crust intact (about 10 cups)

3/4 cup (6 oz/185 g) unsalted butter

2 large yellow onions, about 1 lb (500 g) total weight, finely chopped

11/2 cups (9 oz/280 g) finely chopped celery, including some leafy tops

2 large Granny Smith apples, about 1 lb (500 g) total weight, halved, cored, and diced

2 tablespoons chopped fresh sage or 1 teaspoon dried sage

1 teaspoon dried thyme

1/2 teaspoon freshly grated nutmeg

Salt

1/2 teaspoon freshly ground pepper

1/3 cup (1/2 oz/15 g) minced fresh flat-leaf (Italian) parsley

3 large eggs, lightly beaten

21/2 cups (20 fl oz/625 ml) chicken stock or reduced-sodium chicken broth

The sweet-tart character of Granny Smith apples combines with the tang of sourdough bread in this moist, flavorful stuffing. The crusts add a nice chewiness, but if you prefer, you may cut them off.

Preheat the oven to 250°F (120°C). Spread the bread cubes on 2 rimmed baking sheets and dry in the oven for 40 minutes. Remove from the oven and set aside. Raise the oven temperature to 375°F (190°C).

In a large frying pan over medium heat, melt 3 tablespoons of the butter. Add the onions and celery and sauté until soft, about 10 minutes. Transfer to a large bowl. In the same frying pan, melt 2 tablespoons of the butter, add the apples, and sauté until glazed, about 5 minutes. Transfer to the bowl holding the onion-celery mixture. Add the sage, thyme, nutmeg, salt to taste, and the pepper and mix well. Again in the same frying pan, melt the remaining butter, add the bread cubes and parsley, and toss to coat. Transfer to the bowl. In another bowl, combine the eggs and stock and whisk until blended. Pour the stock mixture over the bread mixture and toss gently.

Transfer the stuffing to a lightly buttered 4-qt (4-l) baking dish, cover tightly with aluminum foil, and bake for 30 minutes. Uncover and continue to bake until the stuffing is hot throughout and lightly browned and crisp on top, 20–30 minutes longer. Serve hot.

Serves 8–10

WILD RICE AND LEEK PILAF

This flavorful pilaf can be prepared on the stove top or baked in the oven. If you like, add ½ cup (3 oz/90 g) golden raisins or dried cranberries to the wild rice at the beginning of cooking and finish the dish with a sprinkling of toasted slivered almonds.

In a large saucepan over medium heat, warm the olive oil. Add the leek and onion and sauté until soft, 8–10 minutes. Add the wild rice, thyme, and salt and season to taste with pepper. Pour in the stock, bring to a boil, reduce the heat to medium-low, cover, and cook until the wild rice is tender, about 50 minutes.

Transfer to a warmed serving bowl and serve hot.

Serves 8–10

3 tablespoons olive oil or unsalted butter

1 large leek, white and tender green parts, halved lengthwise and thinly sliced crosswise

½ cup (2½ oz/75 g) finely chopped yellow onion

2 cups (12 oz/375 g) wild rice

1 teaspoon dried thyme

¾ teaspoon salt

Freshly ground pepper

6 cups (48 fl oz/1.5 l) chicken or turkey stock or reduced-sodium chicken broth

ANISE HONEY WREATH LOAVES

If you prefer, you can infuse the milk with lavender in place of the aniseeds. The decorative ring shape is especially nice for slicing into even wedges. This bread is excellent served at room temperature or toasted.

2¹/₂ teaspoons (1 package) active dry yeast

¹/₂ cup (4 fl oz/125 ml) warm water (105°–115°F/40°–46°C)

Pinch of sugar

2 tablespoons aniseeds or 3 tablespoons dried lavender flowers

1 cup (8 fl oz/250 ml) whole milk

¹/₃ cup (3 fl oz/80 ml) extra-virgin olive oil

¹/₃ cup (4 oz/125 g) honey

2 teaspoons salt

2 whole large eggs plus 1 large egg, separated

1 tablespoon brandy or Cognac

Grated zest of 2 lemons

About 4¹/₂ cups (22¹/₂ oz/705 g) unbleached all-purpose (plain) flour

¹/₃ cup (1¹/₂ oz/45 g) pine nuts

Sprinkle the yeast into the warm water, add the sugar, and let stand until bubbly, about 10 minutes. Crush the aniseeds in a mortar with a pestle. In a small saucepan over medium heat, combine the milk and aniseeds and heat until steaming and bubbles appear on the surface, about 5 minutes. Remove from the heat and let cool to lukewarm. Strain through a fine-mesh sieve.

In the bowl of a stand mixer fitted with the paddle attachment, or in a large bowl using a wooden spoon, combine the flavored milk, olive oil, honey, and salt. Add the 2 whole eggs, 1 egg yolk, brandy, lemon zest, and 1 cup (5 oz/155 g) of the flour and beat on low speed or by hand until smooth and creamy. Add the yeast mixture and another 1 cup of the flour and beat until smooth. Add the remaining flour ¹/₂ cup (2¹/₂ oz/75 g) at a time, beating well after each addition and adding just enough to make a soft dough. Switch to the dough hook and knead for about 10 minutes. Alternatively, transfer the dough to a lightly floured work surface and knead by hand for about 10 minutes. The dough should be smooth, satiny, and soft but not sticky. Shape into a ball, place in a large oiled bowl, and turn the ball to coat the surface. Cover the bowl with plastic wrap and let the dough rise in a warm place until doubled in size, about 2 hours.

Oil 2 rimmed baking sheets. Transfer the risen dough to a lightly floured work surface and knead lightly. Divide in half and shape each piece into a round ball. With your fingers, poke a hole in the center of each dough ball and stretch it into a ring shape about 10 inches (25 cm) in diameter. Transfer to the prepared baking sheets. Cover with plastic wrap and let rise until doubled in size, about 1 hour.

Position 2 racks in the middle of the oven and preheat to 350°F (180°C).

Lightly beat the remaining egg white and brush it over the dough rounds. Sprinkle with the pine nuts. Bake, switching the pans between the racks and rotating them 180 degrees at the midway point, until the loaves are golden brown and sound hollow when thumped, 25–30 minutes. Let cool on wire racks. Cut into wedges and serve warm or at room temperature.

Makes 2 ring-shaped loaves; serves 8–10

WALNUT-PRALINE PUMPKIN PIE

A crunchy nut glaze seals the top of this spicy pumpkin custard pie. Make the pastry a day in advance of the pie to expedite assembly later. If you like, top each wedge of pie with a dollop of whipped cream flavored with maple syrup.

Preheat the oven to 425°F (220°C).

To make the pastry, in a food processor or in a bowl, combine the flour, granulated sugar, and butter. Pulse or cut in the butter with a pastry blender until the mixture resembles fine crumbs. Add the egg yolk and pulse or toss with a fork until blended. Add the ice water and process or mix just until the dough clings together in a ball.

On a lightly floured work surface, roll out the dough into a round 12 inches (30 cm) in diameter. Drape the pastry round over the rolling pin and carefully transfer it to a 9-inch (23-cm) pie dish. Ease it into the dish, pressing it into the bottom and up the sides. Trim the overhang to 1 inch (2.5 cm), then fold the excess dough under the overhang and flute the edges. Refrigerate until firm, about 20 minutes or up to overnight.

Bake for 8 minutes. Remove from the oven and reduce the oven temperature to 375°F (190°C). Let the pastry shell cool on a wire rack until ready to fill.

To make the filling, in a large bowl, beat the eggs until blended. Add the brown sugar, cinnamon, ginger, cloves, nutmeg, and salt and mix well. Stir in the pumpkin purée and half-and-half. Pour into the pastry shell. Bake for 35 minutes.

Meanwhile, to make the topping, in a bowl, combine the nuts and brown sugar, mixing well.

After the pie has baked for 35 minutes, sprinkle the topping around the perimeter of the surface. Continue to bake until a knife inserted into the center comes out clean, about 5 minutes longer. Remove from the oven, turn the oven to the broiler (grill) setting, and broil (grill) the pie for 30 seconds to caramelize the brown sugar. Watch the pie carefully to avoid scorching.

Serve warm or at room temperature.

Serves 8–10

PASTRY

1¼ cups (6½ oz/200 g) all-purpose (plain) flour

1 tablespoon granulated sugar

½ cup (4 oz/125 g) cold unsalted butter, cut into ½-inch (12-mm) pieces

1 large egg yolk

1½ tablespoons ice water

FILLING

3 large eggs

¾ cup (6 oz/185 g) firmly packed light brown sugar

½ teaspoon ground cinnamon

½ teaspoon ground ginger

¼ teaspoon ground cloves

¼ teaspoon freshly grated nutmeg

½ teaspoon salt

1⅔ cups (13 oz/410 g) pumpkin purée

1½ cups (12 fl oz/375 ml) half-and-half (half cream) or whole milk

NUT TOPPING

1½ cups (6 oz/185 g) walnuts or pecans, chopped

⅓ cup (2½ oz/75 g) firmly packed light brown sugar

PEAR TART TATIN WITH BRANDIED CREAM

For this decorative open-face tart, select firm but ripe Anjou or Bosc pears for the best baking. Pear brandy heightens the flavor of the fruit and laces the whipped cream topping.

PASTRY

1¼ cups (6½ oz/200 g) all-purpose (plain) flour

1 tablespoon granulated sugar

⅛ teaspoon salt

5 tablespoons (2½ oz/75 g) cold unsalted butter, cut into ½-inch (12-mm) pieces

2 tablespoons cold solid vegetable shortening

3 tablespoons ice water

FILLING

3 large, firm but ripe Anjou or Bosc pears, about 2 lb (1 kg) total weight

2½ tablespoons pear brandy or Cognac

2 tablespoons unsalted butter

½ cup (4 oz/125 g) granulated sugar

1 teaspoon light corn syrup

Freshly grated nutmeg

BRANDIED CREAM

½ cup (4 fl oz/125 ml) heavy (double) cream

2 tablespoons confectioners' (icing) sugar, sifted

2 tablespoons pear brandy or Cognac

To make the pastry, in a food processor, combine the flour, granulated sugar, salt, butter, and shortening. Pulse until the butter pieces are the size of peas. Sprinkle with the ice water and pulse 3 or 4 times to incorporate. Transfer to a lightly floured surface and knead into a ball. Wrap in plastic wrap and refrigerate for 30 minutes.

Preheat the oven to 400°F (200°C). Peel, halve, and core the pears lengthwise and cut each half in half again; you should have 12 pieces of pear. Place in a bowl, add the pear brandy, and toss gently. Set aside.

On a lightly floured work surface, roll out the dough into a round 10 inches (25 cm) in diameter. Drape the pastry round over the rolling pin, transfer to a baking sheet, and refrigerate for 20 minutes.

In a 10-inch (25-cm) ovenproof frying pan over medium-high heat, melt the butter. Stir in the granulated sugar and corn syrup and cook, stirring occasionally and shaking the pan, until the syrup turns a golden amber, about 7 minutes. Remove from the heat and arrange the pear quarters, cut side down, in the pan in a pinwheel design. Sprinkle lightly with nutmeg. Lay the chilled pastry round over the top and cut 3 slits to let the steam escape. Tuck the edges of the pastry down slightly between the pears and the pan rim to make a pretty fluted edge.

Bake until the pastry is golden brown and the pears are tender (test with a knife tip through a slit in the top), about 30 minutes. Remove from the oven and let cool for 1 minute. Invert a large serving plate on top of the pan. Holding the pan and the plate firmly, quickly invert them together. Lift off the pan, revealing the pears on top. Spoon any extra caramel from the pan over the pears.

To make the brandied cream, using an electric mixer on medium-high speed, beat the cream until soft peaks form. Fold in the confectioners' sugar and brandy. Serve the tart warm or at room temperature with the whipped cream.

Serves 8–10

PECAN PRALINE PIE

SOUTHERN THANKSGIVING

No matter where you live, Thanksgiving can be the perfect occasion to evoke the refined elegance and soul-satisfying abundance of traditional southern hospitality. In place of turkey, this lavish buffet menu features a glazed ham served with all its typical accompaniments. It is a feast fit for your finest silver, china, and table linens, and for the

best crystal in the house. Use lush, yet restrained floral arrangements to set the mood, lining the center of the table with low white vases, each brimming with a single type of bloom. Choose flowers in shades of dusky purple, green, and mauve, and add accents of hanging greenery to create a look of southern opulence.

TIPS FOR A FORMAL THANKSGIVING

- Use high-quality white or off-white linens. The tablecloth and napkins do not have to be a perfect color match, but the napkins should be identical.

- Make an attractive place marker or card for each place setting.

- Use silver trays for passing drinks and hors d'oeuvres.

- To add height and sparkle to the buffet, arrange biscuits on a tiered tea tray, and use footed cake pedestals to display desserts.

MENU

Mint Ginger Ale

Cajun Shrimp

— • —

Baked Ham with Honey-Port Glaze

Vidalia Onion Marmalade

Soufflé Spoon Bread with Cheddar Cheese

Carrots Glazed with Mustard and Brown Sugar

Collard Greens Piquant

Cheddar Chive Biscuits

— • —

Apple-Ginger Tart with Cider Bourbon Sauce

Pecan Praline Pie

WORK PLAN

TWO DAYS IN ADVANCE
Make the marmalade

Prepare pastry for the pie and tart

Make sauce for the tart

THE DAY OF THE MEAL
Prepare the shrimp and spoon bread

Bake the ham

Bake the biscuits, pie, and tart

JUST BEFORE SERVING
Bake the spoon bread

Cook the greens

Cook and glaze the carrots

Pour the ginger ale

HEIRLOOM RECIPE PLACE MARKERS

A treasured recipe tied with a satin ribbon makes an elegant place marker for your guests to take home. Use a recipe from your Thanksgiving menu, or choose a regional specialty or family favorite.

select a recipe to feature, type it up in a classic typeface on the computer, and print one copy for each guest on heavy, cream-colored paper.

roll up each recipe with the printed side facing out. Tie a length of silk ribbon around one of the recipes, trim the ribbon, and then untie it and use it as a guide to cut the remaining ribbons.

tie the ribbons around the recipes. If you like, attach a tag with each guest's name to the ribbon, or write it directly on the recipe. Lay a rolled recipe across each place setting.

Mint Ginger Ale

Of the many varieties of mint, spearmint is the best one to use for this thirst-quencher. For a more sophisticated version, tonic can stand in for the ginger ale, and adults may wish to add a jigger of bourbon.

In a small bowl, using the back of a spoon, crush the mint with the sugar and let stand for 10 minutes. In each individual glass, place a generous $1/2$ teaspoon crushed sugared mint. Add several ice cubes and pour in the ginger ale. If desired, add a splash of bourbon to each glass. Serve immediately.

Serves 8–10

2 tablespoons packed fresh mint leaves, julienned

1 teaspoon sugar

Ice cubes

2 bottles (1 qt/1 l each) ginger ale or tonic water

Bourbon (optional)

Cajun Shrimp

Create this easy appetizer with Bloody Mary mix brightened by fresh cilantro and lemon juice. You can substitute tomato juice cocktail for the mix. If you are serving only adults, add a splash of vodka to the sauce before adding the shrimp.

In a bowl, stir together the Bloody Mary mix, lemon juice, garlic, minced cilantro, Worcestershire sauce, and Tabasco. Season to taste with salt and pepper. Add the shrimp and toss gently to coat. Cover and refrigerate for 30 minutes.

To serve, arrange the shrimp on a platter, garnish with the cilantro sprigs, and accompany with cocktail napkins and toothpicks for easy serving.

Serves 8–10

$3/4$ cup (6 fl oz/180 ml) Bloody Mary mix

2 tablespoons fresh lemon juice

1 clove garlic, minced

2 tablespoons minced fresh cilantro (fresh coriander), plus sprigs for garnish

1 teaspoon Worcestershire sauce

Dash of Tabasco sauce, or to taste

Salt and freshly ground pepper

36 cooked deveined large shrimp (prawns) with tails in place, about $3/4$ lb (375 g) total weight

BAKED HAM WITH HONEY-PORT GLAZE

A fully cooked ham develops a caramel-like glaze in the oven and makes a festive presentation on the holiday table. Although a boneless ham is easy to slice, a bone-in ham offers more succulent flavor.

1 fully cooked bone-in 8-lb (4-kg) ham

1/2 cup (3 1/2 oz/105 g) firmly packed light brown sugar

1/4 cup (3 oz/90 g) honey

2 teaspoons dry mustard

3/4 cup (6 fl oz/180 ml) Port

Position a rack in the lower third of the oven and preheat to 325°F (165°C).

Using a sharp knife, score the fat on the upper half of the ham in a diamond pattern, cutting about 1/4 inch (6 mm) deep. Place the ham fat-side up on a rack in a roasting pan. Roast for 1 1/4 hours.

In a small bowl, mix together the brown sugar, honey, and mustard. Pat half of the sugar mixture over the scored surface of the ham. Stir the Port into the remaining mixture. Continue to roast the ham, basting several times with the Port mixture, until the ham is glazed and shiny, about 1 hour longer.

Transfer the ham to a cutting board. Let rest for 15 minutes or longer before carving.

Serves 8–10

VIDALIA ONION MARMALADE

A relish of caramelized onions is the ideal savory accompaniment to baked ham. This versatile condiment is also excellent with roast turkey, chicken, or lamb or as a spread on cheese-topped crackers.

1/4 cup (2 fl oz/60 ml) extra-virgin olive oil

6 Vidalia or other sweet onions, about 3 lb (1.5 kg) total weight, coarsely chopped

3/4 teaspoon salt

1/4 cup (2 oz/60 g) firmly packed light brown sugar

1/4 cup (2 fl oz/60 ml) white balsamic vinegar

3 tablespoons white wine vinegar

1 tablespoon honey

1 teaspoon dried thyme

Freshly ground pepper

In a large frying pan over medium heat, warm the olive oil. Add the onions and salt and stir to coat with the oil. Cover and cook, stirring occasionally, until the onions are soft and pale gold, about 30 minutes. Stir in the brown sugar, vinegars, honey, and thyme. Season to taste with pepper. Simmer uncovered, stirring occasionally, until the onion juices have evaporated and the mixture is thick, about 30 minutes. Let cool to room temperature for immediate use, or transfer to an airtight container, cover, and refrigerate for up to 3 weeks before serving.

Serves 8–10

Soufflé Spoon Bread with Cheddar Cheese

This popular southern dish, like a sturdy soufflé, is given a boost of flavor by the addition of extra-sharp Cheddar cheese. It makes an excellent accompaniment to ham, game, or turkey. Assemble ahead of time, then bake before serving.

Preheat the oven to 350°F (180°C). Lightly butter a 1½-qt (1.5-l) soufflé dish or baking dish.

Pour the milk into a saucepan and add the salt. Bring to a slow boil, just until bubbles appear on the sides, over medium-high heat and then reduce the heat to a simmer. Stir in the cornmeal and cook, stirring, until it thickens, about 10 minutes. Stir in the butter and nutmeg. Remove from the heat and whisk in the egg yolks and cheese. Set aside to let cool slightly.

Using an electric mixer, beat the egg whites until soft peaks form. Gently fold the beaten whites into the cornmeal mixture just until no white streaks are visible. Transfer to the prepared soufflé dish. (The spoon bread can be assembled up to this point 8 hours in advance of baking. Cover and refrigerate, then bring to room temperature before continuing.)

Bake until puffed and golden brown, 35–40 minutes. Serve hot.

Serves 8–10

2½ cups (20 fl oz/625 ml) whole milk

½ teaspoon salt

½ cup (3½ oz/105 g) white cornmeal

4 tablespoons (2 oz/60 g) unsalted butter

¼ teaspoon freshly grated nutmeg or ground mace

6 large eggs, separated

1 cup (4 oz/125 g) shredded extra-sharp white Cheddar cheese

Carrots Glazed with Mustard and Brown Sugar

Brown sugar caramelized with butter and Dijon mustard creates a sweet-hot glaze for carrots. A sprinkling of fresh chives adds a colorful finish.

Bring a saucepan three-fourths full of water to a boil. Salt the water, add the carrots, and cook until tender, 6–8 minutes. Drain well.

Return the pan of carrots to medium heat. Add the butter, mustard, and brown sugar, season to taste with salt and pepper, and stir gently to coat. Cook, stirring constantly, until the carrots are evenly glazed. Transfer to a warmed serving bowl and sprinkle with the chives. Serve hot.

Serves 8–10

Salt

8 large carrots, peeled and sliced on the diagonal

1 tablespoon unsalted butter

1 tablespoon Dijon mustard

1 tablespoon firmly packed light brown sugar

Freshly ground pepper

1/3 cup (1/2 oz/15 g) coarsely chopped fresh chives or flat-leaf (Italian) parsley

Collard Greens Piquant

A splash of balsamic vinegar gives a lift to slightly bitter greens. Wash the greens thoroughly to remove any sand.

In a large pot over medium heat, warm 1 tablespoon of the olive oil. Add the onion and sauté until soft, about 5 minutes. Add the greens and 2 cups (16 fl oz/500 ml) water. Cover and simmer until tender, about 20 minutes. Drain thoroughly and return the pot of greens to medium heat. Season to taste with salt and pepper. Drizzle with the vinegar and the remaining 3 tablespoons olive oil and heat through, tossing to mingle the flavors. Serve warm.

Serves 8–10

4 tablespoons (2 fl oz/60 ml) extra-virgin olive oil

1 yellow onion, chopped

About 4 lb (2 kg) collard and mustard greens, tough stems removed

Salt and freshly ground pepper

1/4 cup (2 fl oz/60 ml) balsamic vinegar

CHEDDAR CHIVE BISCUITS

Minced chives and shreds of white Cheddar cheese lace these flaky biscuits. The dough is easily mixed by hand or in a stand mixer. To make it with buttermilk instead of milk, decrease the baking powder to 2 teaspoons and add $1/2$ teaspoon baking soda (bicarbonate of soda).

Preheat the oven to 425°F (220°C). Lightly butter a rimmed baking sheet.

To make the dough by hand, in a large bowl, stir together the flour, baking powder, salt, cheese, and chives. Using a pastry blender or 2 knives, cut the butter into the flour mixture until it resembles coarse crumbs. Pour in the milk and mix with a fork or rubber spatula just until the dry ingredients are evenly moistened. Transfer the dough to a lightly floured work surface and knead gently a few times until the dough clings together.

To make the dough in a stand mixer, combine the flour, baking powder, salt, cheese, and chives in the mixer bowl. Fit the mixer with the paddle attachment and mix on low speed for a few seconds to combine. Add the butter and mix on medium-low speed just until the mixture forms coarse crumbs. Add the milk and mix for a few seconds until evenly moistened. Transfer the dough to a lightly floured work surface and knead gently a few times until the dough clings together.

Roll or pat out the dough about $1/2$ inch (12 mm) thick. Using a 2-inch (5-cm) biscuit cutter or glass dipped in flour, cut out rounds by pressing straight down and lifting straight up. Do not twist the cutter or glass or the biscuits may become lopsided. Alternatively, roll or pat out the dough into a rectangle and cut into 2-inch (5-cm) squares. Place the biscuits 1 inch (2.5 cm) apart on the prepared baking sheet.

Bake until golden brown on the edges, 15–18 minutes. Remove from the oven, transfer to a wire rack, and let cool for 10 minutes. Serve warm.

Makes about 18 biscuits; serves 8–10

2 cups (10 oz/315 g) all-purpose (plain) flour

$2^1/2$ teaspoons baking powder

$1/2$ teaspoon salt

$3/4$ cup (3 oz/90 g) shredded white Cheddar cheese

$1/3$ cup ($1/2$ oz/15 g) minced fresh chives

6 tablespoons (3 oz/90 g) cold unsalted butter, cut into chunks

$3/4$ cup (6 fl oz/180 ml) whole milk

APPLE-GINGER TART WITH CIDER BOURBON SAUCE

A warm bourbon sauce is the perfect complement to this streusel-topped apple tart. It can be made in advance and reheated over low heat just before serving. You can also make a variation with Anjou or Bosc pears in place of the apples; decrease the baking time by 15 minutes.

Preheat the oven to 425°F (220°C).

To make the pastry, in a food processor, combine the flour, butter, and confectioners' sugar. Pulse until fine crumbs form. Measure out $^1/_3$ cup ($^3/_4$ oz/20g) of the crumb mixture and set aside.

Pat the remaining crumb mixture evenly on the bottom and up the sides of an 11-inch (28-cm) tart pan with a removable bottom. Refrigerate or freeze the tart shell for 10 minutes. Bake until the crumb mixture just begins to brown, about 6 minutes. Let cool completely on a wire rack.

To make the filling, halve and core the unpeeled apples and then thinly slice. In a small bowl, mix together the reserved crumb mixture and the brown sugar. In a large bowl, combine the apple slices, granulated sugar, lemon juice, ginger, and cinnamon. Toss to coat the apples. Pile the filling into the cooled pastry shell. Sprinkle with the brown sugar mixture.

Bake for 15 minutes. Reduce the oven temperature to 375°F (190°C) and continue to bake until the apples are tender when pierced with a knife, 45–50 minutes longer. Cover the top with aluminum foil during the last 30 minutes to prevent the top from browning too much. Transfer to a wire rack and let cool.

To make the sauce, in a small saucepan over medium heat, combine the brown sugar and cornstarch, stirring to remove any lumps. Stir in the apple cider and salt. Raise the heat to medium-high and bring to a boil, stirring constantly. Cook until thickened, about 4 minutes. Reduce the heat to medium, stir in the butter and bourbon, and simmer just until well blended.

Cut the tart into wedges to serve. Drizzle a little of the hot sauce over each wedge.

Serves 8–10

PASTRY

1$^1/_4$ cups (6$^1/_2$ oz/200 g) all-purpose (plain) flour

10 tablespoons (5 oz/155 g) cold unsalted butter

2 tablespoons confectioners' (icing) sugar

FILLING

8 Granny Smith or Golden Delicious apples, about 3 lb (1.5 kg) total weight

$^1/_3$ cup (2$^1/_2$ oz/75 g) firmly packed light brown sugar

$^1/_4$ cup (2 oz/60 g) granulated sugar

3 tablespoons fresh lemon juice

6 tablespoons (2 oz/60 g) finely chopped crystallized ginger

1 teaspoon ground cinnamon

CIDER-BOURBON SAUCE

1 cup (7 oz/220 g) firmly packed light brown sugar

2 tablespoons cornstarch (cornflour)

2 cups (16 fl oz/500 ml) apple cider

Pinch of salt

4 tablespoons (2 oz/60 g) unsalted butter

$^1/_2$ cup (4 fl oz/125 ml) bourbon

PECAN PRALINE PIE

A caramelized topping of pecan praline embellishes this classic southern favorite. Don't be intimidated by the crust; this pastry is easy to handle. You can also make the pastry and line the dish up to a day ahead. Wrap the lined dish tightly in plastic wrap and refrigerate until ready to bake.

Preheat the oven to 400°F (200°C).

To make the pastry, in a food processor, combine the flour, granulated sugar, and butter and process until the mixture resembles fine crumbs. Add the egg yolk and pulse until blended. Add the ice water and pulse just until the dough forms a ball. To make the pastry by hand, in a bowl, stir together the flour and granulated sugar. Using a pastry blender or 2 knives, cut the butter into the flour mixture until it resembles fine crumbs. Add the egg yolk and mix with a fork until blended. Gradually add the ice water and mix just until the dough forms a ball.

On a lightly floured work surface, roll out the dough into a round 12 inches (30 cm) in diameter. Drape the round over the rolling pin, transfer it to a 9-inch (23-cm) pie dish, and ease it into the bottom and up the sides. Trim the edges, leaving a 1-inch (2.5-cm) overhang. Turn under the overhang and flute the edges. Refrigerate the shell until firm, about 30 minutes or up to overnight. Line it with aluminum foil and fill with pie weights or dried beans. Bake for 15–20 minutes; the shell should be dry and still pale. Remove the weights and foil. Let the shell cool on a wire rack. Reduce the oven temperature to 350°F (180°C).

To make the filling, in a large bowl, beat the eggs with a whisk. Add the corn syrup, brown sugar, molasses, melted butter, Cognac, and salt and whisk until smooth. Scatter the chopped pecans evenly in the cooled pastry shell. Pour the egg mixture over the nuts. Bake until the top is browned, the filling is almost set, and a knife inserted into the center comes out almost clean, 45–50 minutes. Let cool on a wire rack to room temperature.

To make the topping, in a small saucepan over medium heat, melt the butter. Add the pecans, sprinkle with the granulated sugar, and heat, stirring, until the nuts are toasted and caramelized, about 15 minutes. Pour onto a plate, spread into a single layer, and let cool. Scatter over the top of the pie. To serve, cut the pie into wedges and top with a dollop of whipped cream.

Serves 8–10

PASTRY

1¹/₄ cups (6¹/₂ oz/200 g) all-purpose (plain) flour

1 tablespoon granulated sugar

¹/₂ cup (4 oz/125 g) unsalted butter, cut into ¹/₂-inch (12-mm) pieces

1 large egg yolk

1¹/₂ tablespoons ice water

FILLING

3 large eggs

³/₄ cup (7¹/₂ fl oz/235 ml) dark corn syrup

²/₃ cup (5 oz/155 g) firmly packed light brown sugar

¹/₄ cup (3 oz/90 g) unsulfured light molasses

¹/₄ cup (2 oz/60 g) unsalted butter, melted and slightly cooled

1 tablespoon Cognac

¹/₄ teaspoon salt

1³/₄ cups (7 oz/220 g) coarsely chopped pecans

PRALINE PECAN TOPPING

2 tablespoons unsalted butter

1¹/₂ cups (6 oz/185 g) coarsely chopped pecans

¹/₄ cup (2 oz/60 g) granulated sugar

Whipped cream flavored with Cognac for serving

DAY-AFTER LUNCH

After all the feasting and fun, Thanksgiving Friday is a relaxing time to unwind with friends and relatives. It is an ideal moment for a cozy lunch in the family room, where everyone can enjoy a casual, self-serve spread while watching sports on television and catching up. This menu works particularly well for drop-in entertaining. Set up a station in the kitchen with sandwiches, salad, and drinks along with plates and trays. Arrange the dips and nibbles

on platters on the coffee table, restocking them as needed throughout the afternoon. When it's time for dessert, bring out the brownies, along with bowls of fruit and freshly brewed coffee and tea.

MENU

Cranberry Lemonade

Gorgonzola Dip with Crudités

— • —

Crab and Shrimp Spread

Waldorf Salad with Cranberries and Walnuts

*Italian Loaf with Turkey, White Cheddar,
and Cranberry Sauce*

— • —

Extra-Rich Sheet Brownies

TIPS FOR GAME DAY ENTERTAINING

- Bundle silverware in casual napkins, and tuck a colorful autumn leaf into each bundle.

- Set up a self-serve beverage station in the kitchen with pitchers of the lemonade and a cooler or ice tub stocked with sparkling water, sodas, and juice.

- Offer trays or folding tables to make eating easier.

- Create a separate seating area away from the television for guests who don't want to watch the games.

- Keep a supply of disposable plates and cups on hand for kids to use.

WORK PLAN

UP TO TWO DAYS IN ADVANCE

Prepare the sugar syrup for
the lemonade

Mix the cheese dip

Bake the brownies

THE MORNING OF THE LUNCH

Prepare the crudités

Mix the shellfish spread

Assemble the sandwich loaf

Prepare the salad

JUST BEFORE SERVING

Assemble the crudité platter

Finish the lemonade

FALL-COLOR TRAY LINERS

Autumn leaves pressed between sheets of waxed paper are an easy way to dress up and protect the surface of a serving tray. Choose large, uniform rectangular trays with raised edges to hold the liners in place.

collect multicolored fall leaves in varying shapes and sizes. Cut a sheet of waxed paper to fit the bottom of a tray, then use it as a template for cutting more sheets, allowing two per tray.

arrange leaves in an attractive pattern on a sheet of waxed paper and cover with another sheet. Place on an ironing board or heatproof work surface; you may want to cover the surface with a smooth dish towel to protect it.

iron the waxed paper on the low-heat setting until the two sheets stick together.

line each tray with a finished liner, and stack the trays on the buffet.

juice lemons, rolling them under the palm of your hand on the countertop to increase their yield before cutting them. Add the juice to the sugar syrup, let cool, pour the mixture into a pitcher, and chill.

pour the cranberry lemonade into tall, ice-filled glasses arranged on a napkin-lined serving tray.

add the cranberry juice to the pitcher holding the lemon-syrup mixture and stir until thoroughly combined.

garnish each drink with 1 or 2 thin lemon slices and a fresh mint sprig.

CRANBERRY LEMONADE

A simple sugar syrup and freshly squeezed lemon juice give this ruby beverage the best flavor. To save time, you can use 2½ cups (20 fl oz/625 ml) bottled lemonade instead.

6 tablespoons (3 oz/90 g) sugar

3/4 cup (6 fl oz/180 ml) fresh lemon juice

3 cups (24 fl oz/750 ml) cranberry juice

Ice cubes

Fresh mint sprigs and lemon slices for garnish

In a saucepan over medium heat, combine the sugar and 1½ cups (12 fl oz/375 ml) water and cook, stirring to dissolve the sugar. Bring to a boil and cook until the syrup is clear, about 5 minutes. Remove from the heat and stir in the lemon juice. Let cool and then pour into a pitcher and refrigerate until thoroughly chilled.

Stir the cranberry juice into the lemon juice mixture. Add ice cubes to each glass and pour in the lemonade. Garnish with mint sprigs and lemon slices.

Serves 6–8

GORGONZOLA DIP WITH CRUDITÉS

This zesty cheese dip is delicious with a variety of fresh vegetables. You can make it in advance, as it keeps well refrigerated for up to four days. Serve the dip in a bowl surrounded by vegetables arranged on a platter.

In a food processor, combine the shallot, parsley, chives, tarragon, sour cream, yogurt, mustard, and vinegar and process until blended. Add the cheese and process for a few seconds to distribute evenly. Transfer to a serving bowl, cover, and refrigerate until well chilled.

Just before serving, top the dip with a scattering of crumbled blue cheese. Arrange the raw vegetables on a platter or in a basket and serve accompanied with the dip.

Serves 6–8

1 shallot, chopped

1/4 cup (1/3 oz/10 g) minced fresh flat-leaf (Italian) parsley

1/4 cup (1/3 oz/10 g) minced fresh chives

2 teaspoons minced fresh tarragon, or 1/2 teaspoon dried tarragon

1 cup (8 oz/250 g) sour cream

1 cup (8 oz/250 g) plain yogurt

1 teaspoon Dijon mustard

1 tablespoon white balsamic vinegar

2 oz (60 g) Gorgonzola or other blue-veined cheese, crumbled (about 1/2 cup), plus more for garnish

Mix of raw vegetables

CRAB AND SHRIMP SPREAD

A seafood spread is a welcome addition to the post-Thanksgiving menu. This creamy version is fast to assemble and is especially good atop lahvosh or other crackers or toasted thin baguette slices.

In a bowl, combine the cream cheese, sour cream, lemon juice, lemon zest, Worcestershire sauce, and Tabasco and mix together until blended. Stir in the chives, minced parsley, celery, shrimp, and crabmeat. Transfer to a serving bowl, cover, and refrigerate until well chilled.

To serve, garnish with parsley sprigs and serve with crackers and/or baguette slices.

Serves 6–8

1/2 lb (250 g) cream cheese, at room temperature

1/4 cup (2 oz/60 g) sour cream or 1/4 cup (2 fl oz/60 ml) mayonnaise

2 tablespoons fresh lemon juice

2 teaspoons grated lemon zest

1 teaspoon Worcestershire sauce

1/8 teaspoon Tabasco sauce

3 tablespoons minced fresh chives or green (spring) onion tops

3 tablespoons minced fresh flat-leaf (Italian) parsley, plus sprigs for garnish

1/2 cup (3 oz/90 g) minced celery

1/4 lb (125 g) small cooked shrimp (prawns)

3 oz (90 g) fresh-cooked crabmeat, picked over for cartilage and shells

Lahvosh crackers and/or baguette slices

WALDORF SALAD WITH CRANBERRIES AND WALNUTS

The traditional Waldorf salad gets a holiday twist with the addition of dried cranberries and a drizzling of sherry vinegar and fragrant walnut oil in place of mayonnaise.

Preheat the oven to 350°F (180°C). Spread the walnuts on a rimmed baking sheet and bake until lightly toasted and fragrant, 8–10 minutes. Pour onto a plate to cool and then chop coarsely.

Halve and core the apples and cut into $1/2$-inch (12-mm) dice. In a large bowl, toss the apples with the lemon juice. Add the celery, green onions, cranberries, and toasted walnuts. Drizzle with the walnut oil and vinegar. Toss to mix well. Serve at once or cover and refrigerate until serving time.

Serves 6–8

$1/2$ cup (2 oz/60 g) walnuts

2 large Fuji apples, about 1 lb (500 g) total weight, unpeeled

2 large Granny Smith apples, about 1 lb (500 g) total weight, unpeeled

2 tablespoons fresh lemon juice

1 cup (5 oz/155 g) diced celery

2 green (spring) onions, including tender green tops, chopped

$1/2$ cup (2 oz/60 g) dried cranberries

$1/3$ cup (3 fl oz/80 ml) walnut oil

3 tablespoons sherry vinegar or white balsamic vinegar

Italian Loaf with Turkey, White Cheddar, and Cranberry Sauce

Ciabatta or focaccia makes an ideal backdrop for this flavorful sandwich, made from leftover roast turkey (and cranberry sauce, if you have it). Using a whole loaf makes quick work of serving a crowd. It's best made at least one hour ahead, so can be ready well before your guests arrive.

In a small bowl, stir together the mayonnaise and green onions, mixing well. Cut the *ciabatta* in half horizontally, and spread the cut sides with the mayonnaise mixture. Spread 1 side of the bread with the cranberry sauce. Top with the turkey and cheese slices and the arugula. Cover with the other bread half. Wrap tightly in plastic wrap and refrigerate for at least 1 hour or up to 4 hours to allow the flavors to mingle and hold the loaf together for easy slicing.

To serve, cut the loaf into slices 2 inches (5 cm) wide, or place on a wooden cutting board and allow guests to slice and serve the sandwich themselves.

Serves 6–8

1 cup (8 fl oz/250 ml) mayonnaise

4 green (spring) onions, including tender green tops, minced

1 loaf *ciabatta*, about 6 inches (15 cm) wide and 12–14 inches (30–35 cm) long

1 jar (9 oz/220 g) whole-berry cranberry sauce

3/4–1 lb (375–500 g) sliced roast turkey breast

1/4 lb (125 g) sliced white Cheddar cheese

3 cups (3 oz/90 g) arugula (rocket)

Extra-Rich Sheet Brownies

A big panful of brownies always comes in handy for entertaining guests over the Thanksgiving weekend. These are easily varied with different nuts, such as pecans, pistachios, or macadamias.

1¼ cups (5 oz/155 g) walnuts

8 oz (250 g) bittersweet or semisweet (plain) chocolate, coarsely chopped

1 cup (8 oz/250 g) unsalted butter, cut into chunks

1¼ cups (6½ oz/200 g) all-purpose (plain) flour

²⁄₃ cup (2 oz/60 g) unsweetened cocoa powder

2 teaspoons espresso powder or instant coffee powder

1½ teaspoons baking powder

¼ teaspoon salt

6 large eggs

2 cups (1 lb/500 g) sugar

2 teaspoons vanilla extract (essence)

Preheat the oven to 350°F (180°C). Line the bottom and sides of a 10-by-15-inch (25-by-38-cm) baking pan with aluminum foil, shiny side up. Lightly butter the foil.

Spread the walnuts on a rimmed baking sheet and bake until lightly toasted and fragrant, 8–10 minutes. Pour onto a plate to cool and then chop coarsely. Leave the oven on.

Place the chocolate and butter in the top pan of a double boiler and set over (but not touching) barely simmering water in the bottom pan. As they melt, stir occasionally with a wooden spoon. When fully melted, stir to blend and then remove from the heat and let cool slightly.

In a bowl, stir together the flour, cocoa powder, espresso powder, baking powder, and salt. Set aside. In a large bowl, using a wire whisk or an electric mixer on high speed, beat the eggs until light pale yellow. Add the sugar and vanilla and beat until well combined. Stir in the melted chocolate mixture and the flour mixture. Add ¾ cup (3 oz/90 g) of the walnuts and stir to distribute evenly. Spread the mixture in the prepared baking pan. Finely chop the remaining nuts and sprinkle them evenly over the top.

Bake just until barely set and a toothpick inserted into the center of the brownies comes out with crumbs clinging to it, 25–30 minutes. Let cool completely in the pan on a wire rack. Invert the pan onto the rack, lift off the pan, and peel off the foil. Transfer to a cutting board and cut into 2¹⁄₂-inch (6-cm) squares. Store in an airtight container for up to 2 days.

Makes 24 brownies

WEEKEND BREAKFAST

A leisurely Thanksgiving-weekend breakfast is a nice way to extend the holiday, especially if you have a houseful of out-of-town visitors. You can bake the quick bread and set the table the night before, making this a low-stress way to entertain. The menu offers a generous mix of light and hearty items, guaranteeing that all your guests will find

something they like. It can be served family style in the dining room or at the kitchen table, with the food set out on a nearby counter or island. Plates, place mats, and napkins in neutral earthy tones offset by warm accents of wood, wheat, and autumn fruits create a harvest mood.

TIPS FOR A HOLIDAY BREAKFAST

- Greet guests with coffee and smoothies in the kitchen, so you can socialize while putting the finishing touches on the food.

- Serve smoothies in cocktail glasses or wineglasses to give them a touch of refinement.

- Have a selection of juices and herbal teas on hand for guests who prefer to avoid caffeine.

- Fill a tiered serving dish with seasonal fruit and nuts to make an edible buffet centerpiece.

- Briefly warm maple syrup in a heatproof pitcher or dish in the microwave just before serving.

MENU

Cappuccino with Cinnamon and Chocolate

Pumpkin Bread with Orange Cream Cheese

———•———

Seasonal Fruit Platter

Banana Orange Smoothies

———•———

Gruyère and Prosciutto Oven Omelet

Canadian Bacon

Baked French Toast

WORK PLAN

UP TO THREE DAYS IN ADVANCE

Bake the quick bread

THE MORNING OF THE BREAKFAST

Assemble the fruit platter

Assemble the omelet

JUST BEFORE SERVING

Bake the omelet

Prepare the cappuccinos

Blend the smoothies

Bake the French toast

Cook the bacon

Autumn Harvest Centerpiece

Sprays of dried wheat and grasses, arranged in simple terra-cotta flowerpots, are an attractive seasonal decoration that can be clustered together on the table or used to dress up the buffet. At the end of the meal, offer each guest a pot to take home.

gather a variety of dried wheat and other decorative plants and grasses, such as rice stalks and lavender (available at floral supply stores), and a pair of garden shears.

fill terra-cotta pots of varying sizes with floral foam, trimming the foam as needed for a snug fit. Starting at the center, insert one stalk at a time into the foam.

add more stalks, working your way out from the center in a circular pattern, until you have achieved a pleasing symmetry and fullness. Place the pots on the table, grouping them in a balanced arrangement.

make individual shots of espresso using an espresso machine. Pour into small bowls or traditional cappuccino cups.

top each bowl with a dollop of the foam, gently pouring or spooning it from the pitcher onto the surface of the coffee.

pour steamed or frothed milk over the espresso, filling each bowl to within 1/2 inch (12 mm) of the rim. Use a spoon to keep most of the foam in the pitcher.

grate chocolate over the top of each cappuccino with a vegetable peeler, then sprinkle lightly with ground cinnamon.

CAPPUCCINO WITH CINNAMON AND CHOCOLATE

An espresso machine is designed to both brew coffee and steam milk to create frothy cappuccino drinks in short order. If you don't have one, brew up double-strength coffee in place of the espresso and use an immersion blender to whip up hot milk into a fine foam. The best milk for foaming is nonfat. A good cappuccino is composed of equal parts espresso, hot milk, and foam.

6–8 tablespoons (2^1/$_2$–3^1/$_2$ oz/75–105 g) ground dark-roast coffee for brewing espresso, or 3 cups (24 fl oz/750 ml) hot double-strength brewed coffee

3 cups (24 fl oz/750 ml) nonfat milk

Ground cinnamon

3-oz (90-g) piece bittersweet chocolate

With an espresso machine, following the manufacturer's instructions, use the ground coffee to brew 6–8 shots of espresso, one at a time. Separately, again using the machine, steam the milk until foaming. (Alternatively, pour the milk into a microwave-proof 4-cup/32–fl oz/1-l glass container and microwave on high for 2^1/$_2$–3 minutes, or until hot. Using an immersion blender, foam the hot milk.)

Pour the brewed espresso into cups or small bowls, filling each one-third full. Pour in the foaming milk. Sprinkle with cinnamon. Using a vegetable peeler, grate the chocolate over the top.

Serves 6–8

Pumpkin Bread with Orange Cream Cheese

This tender quick bread comes together with a flourish for a breakfast treat or a welcome sweet at any time of day. Sunflower seeds make a decorative topping, and cornmeal lends a nice crunch. You can bake the loaf up to three days in advance, wrap tightly in plastic wrap, and store at room temperature.

Preheat the oven to 350°F (180°C). Lightly butter a 5-by-9-inch (13-by-23-cm) loaf pan.

In a bowl, whisk together the flour, cornmeal, baking soda, salt, cinnamon, ginger, and cloves. In a large bowl, combine the eggs, granulated sugar, brown sugar, oil, yogurt, and pumpkin purée. Beat with a large whisk or an electric mixer on medium speed until smooth, about 1 minute. Stir in the raisins. Add the dry ingredients in 2 batches, mixing just until blended after each addition. Using a rubber spatula, scrape the batter into the prepared pan and smooth the top. Sprinkle with the sunflower seeds.

Bake until a toothpick inserted into the center comes out clean, about 1 hour. If the top starts to brown too much, cover with aluminum foil for the last few minutes. Let cool in the pan on a wire rack for 10 minutes, and then remove from the pan and let cool completely on the wire rack.

To make the orange cream cheese, in a small bowl, combine the cream cheese, sour cream, granulated sugar, and orange zest and mix together until blended. Transfer to a small serving bowl.

To serve, slice the bread into slices $^1/_2$ inch (12 mm) thick and accompany with the orange cream cheese.

Makes 1 loaf; serves 6–8

$1^1/_4$ cups ($6^1/_2$ oz/200 g) all-purpose (plain) flour

$^1/_3$ cup ($1^1/_2$ oz/45 g) white or yellow cornmeal

1 teaspoon baking soda (bicarbonate of soda)

$^1/_2$ teaspoon salt

$1^1/_2$ teaspoons ground cinnamon

1 teaspoon ground ginger

$^1/_4$ teaspoon ground cloves

2 large eggs

$^3/_4$ cup (6 oz/185 g) granulated sugar

$^1/_2$ cup ($3^1/_2$ oz/105 g) firmly packed light brown sugar

$^1/_3$ cup (3 fl oz/80 ml) canola oil

$^1/_3$ cup (3 oz/90 g) plain yogurt

1 cup (8 oz/250 g) pumpkin purée

1 cup (6 oz/185 g) raisins

$^1/_4$ cup (1 oz/30 g) sunflower seeds

ORANGE CREAM CHEESE

$^1/_4$ lb (125 g) cream cheese, at room temperature

2 tablespoons sour cream

2 tablespoons granulated sugar

2 teaspoons grated orange zest

SEASONAL FRUIT PLATTER

A colorful array of fruit brightens your breakfast table. As a seasonal substitution for grapes, scatter sparkling pomegranate seeds over the top. Look in specialty-food stores for the gold-fleshed kiwi, a newly marketed variety bearing a mango/melon flavor.

2 navel oranges, about 3/4 lb (375 g) total weight

2 grapefruits, about 3/4 lb (375 g) total weight

4 green or gold kiwifruits, about 6 oz (185 g) total weight, peeled and sliced crosswise

1 lb (500 g) seedless green grapes

Freshly grated nutmeg

Working with 1 orange at a time, and using a sharp knife, cut a slice off both ends of the orange to reveal the flesh. Stand the orange upright on a cutting board and, using the knife, thickly slice off the peel and pith in strips, following the contour of the fruit. Thinly slice the oranges crosswise. Repeat with the grapefruits.

Arrange the sliced oranges, grapefruits, kiwifruits, and grapes on a serving platter. Sprinkle the nutmeg lightly over all. Cover and refrigerate until serving.

Serves 6–8

BANANA ORANGE SMOOTHIES

A sweet-hot touch of fresh ginger lends a nice surprise when sipping this creamy beverage. If you peel and freeze some of the bananas in advance, they give the drink a frosty thickness. In another season, replace the bananas with an equal amount of fresh strawberries or diced mango.

4 bananas

2 cups (16 oz/500 g) plain yogurt

2 oranges, peeled, cut into 1-inch (2.5-cm) chunks, and seeded

1-inch (2.5-cm) piece fresh ginger, peeled and sliced

Peel 2 of the bananas, seal in a zippered plastic bag, and freeze until firm.

Make the smoothies in 2 batches: For the first batch, peel and cut 1 of the remaining bananas into 1-inch (2.5-cm) chunks. Cut 1 of the frozen bananas into 1-inch (2.5-cm) chunks. In a blender, combine the banana chunks, 1 cup (8 oz/250 g) of the yogurt, 1 orange, and half of the ginger. Blend until smooth. Pour into 3 or 4 glasses. Repeat with the remaining ingredients.

Serves 6–8

Gruyère and Prosciutto Oven Omelet

An easy oven-baked omelet goes together in a jiffy to make a hearty main course for guests. Assemble in advance and refrigerate, then top with the bread cubes just before baking. The omelet can rest, lightly covered with aluminum foil to keep hot, while you bake the French toast (page 130). The croutons add a pleasant crunch to the finished wedges.

Preheat the oven to 350°F (180°C). Lightly butter a shallow 1$\frac{1}{2}$-qt (1.5-l) round baking dish, 9$\frac{1}{2}$ inches (24 cm) in diameter.

In a large bowl, beat the eggs until blended. Stir in the milk, salt, nutmeg, prosciutto, and cheese until evenly distributed. Pour the egg mixture into the prepared baking dish. In a small bowl, toss the bread cubes in the olive oil to coat. Scatter the bread cubes evenly over the egg mixture.

Bake until golden brown on top and slightly puffed, 35–40 minutes. Serve hot, cut into wedges.

Serves 6–8

8 large eggs

1 cup (8 fl oz/250 ml) whole milk

1/4 teaspoon salt

1/4 teaspoon freshly grated nutmeg

2 oz (60 g) prosciutto or ham, julienned

2 cups (8 oz/250 g) shredded Gruyère or Swiss cheese

1/2 cup (3 oz/90 g) sourdough French bread cubes (1/2-inch/12-mm cubes)

2 tablespoons extra-virgin olive oil

CANADIAN BACON

Lean, lightly smoked Canadian bacon is a nice change from regular bacon. If you cannot find it thickly sliced, then buy a piece—it comes in cylinders about 4 inches (10 cm) thick in diameter—and slice it yourself, about ½ inch (12 mm) thick, with a sharp knife.

1 lb (500 g) thick-sliced Canadian bacon

Lay the Canadian bacon slices in a single layer in 2 large, cold frying pans, being careful not to crowd the slices. Place the pans over medium heat and cook until the edges of the rounds start to curl and the bacon starts to brown, about 3 minutes. Using tongs, carefully turn the slices over and cook them until browned, about 3 minutes longer.

Transfer the slices to a plate lined with paper towels to drain briefly, then arrange on a warmed serving platter and serve at once.

Serves 6–8

BAKED FRENCH TOAST

An ideal breakfast dish for a busy holiday, this flavorful toast is quickly assembled and bakes in under 15 minutes.

1 cup (8 fl oz/250 ml) half-and-half (half cream) or whole milk

4 large eggs

2 tablespoons firmly packed light brown sugar

½ teaspoon ground cinnamon

¼ teaspoon freshly grated nutmeg

¼ teaspoon salt

12 slices sweet French bread, other white bread, or egg bread

2 tablespoons unsalted butter, melted

Maple syrup for serving

Preheat the oven to 400°F (200°C). Lightly butter a nonstick rimmed baking sheet.

In a bowl, whisk together the half-and-half, eggs, brown sugar, cinnamon, nutmeg, and salt. One slice at a time, turn the bread in the egg mixture to coat on both sides, soaking each slice for about 30 seconds. Shake off the excess batter and transfer the soaked bread to the prepared baking sheet.

Bake until the tops are golden, 5–7 minutes. Flip each slice and continue to bake until puffed and golden on the second side, 5–7 minutes longer.

Turn the oven to the broiler (grill) setting. Brush the tops of the baked toasts with the melted butter. Place under the broiler until lightly browned, about 1 minute. Serve at once with warmed maple syrup.

Serves 6–8

THE THANKSGIVING TABLE

More than any other holiday, Thanksgiving is celebrated with a bountiful table. By assembling the right balance of elements, any table can be made festive and beautiful. Start with something you know you want to use—the family silver, a mix of transferware—and let that be your guide as you consider these five basic categories: dinnerware, glassware, flatware, linens, and decorative elements.

Dinnerware

The plates and serving dishes you choose can help set the overall tone for your celebration. Don't be concerned about all the pieces matching. What is important is that everything has a harmonious style and palette. Even a formal table does not require fine china. Large, plain white dinner plates, available at restaurant-supply stores, are a good choice for both elegant and casual settings. You can augment the plates with colored or patterned serving dishes to create a contemporary or traditional look. Transferware and family heirloom dishes are particularly appropriate for Thanksgiving. If you don't have a complete set, unmatched serving pieces that complement your dishes and tableware can add warmth and charm to the dining table.

Glassware

Well-chosen glassware, even if unadorned and straightforward, lends sparkle and richness to the setting. Simple, classic stemware is always an appropriate choice and works well for either a formal or casual Thanksgiving meal. Setting the table with water glasses and wineglasses that match (the water goes in the larger glass), a practice used in many restaurants, is an easy way to create a sense of elegance. Whether you are serving cocktails in pretty tumblers or hot cider in glass teacups, the basic principle remains the same: Be consistent, assembling glasses of similar quality and style for a given beverage. Even an inexpensive set of glasses can bring a table setting together, because its matching shapes and sizes create a sense of uniformity.

Flatware

When it comes to flatware for the holiday table, mixing and matching is a nice way to add a touch of homey charm, especially if you have an eclectic collection of vintage flatware. Good-quality stainless-steel flatware goes with virtually any setting, from modern and informal to traditional and elegant. Look for heavy pieces with thick handles. If you have a set of family silver, Thanksgiving is the ideal occasion to use it.

Linens

Your choice of linens, including the decision not to use a tablecloth, can define the look of the entire table. For most Thanksgiving settings, understated linens made of high-quality cotton or linen are an excellent choice. You can add color and interest to each place setting by folding or tying the napkin and incorporating a decorative element, such as a spray of foliage or autumn leaf that matches the centerpiece. Your tablecloth and napkins do not need to match, but their style and colors should complement each other. For casual settings, be creative with a variety of colored napkins that fit your overall style.

Decorative Elements

Here is a basic rule for decorating the Thanksgiving table: Repeating patterns create a pleasing effect. This can be achieved by limiting decorations to a few beautiful elements in a few colors. They can be elegant, earthy, antique, modern, refined, or whimsical. You can use virtually anything, from a splendid crystal bowl to a humble terra-cotta flowerpot, as long as the total look remains focused and harmonious.

Choose articles that have a special significance for you and your family, such as an heirloom candelabra or platter. Or, select items that fit the mood of the season, such as fresh or dried flowers, pomegranates, apples, pumpkins and squashes, nuts, autumn leaves and branches, and sheaves of wheat. Use a few of these to create a centerpiece, to adorn a central table runner, to add an accent to each place setting, and,

if you wish, to decorate the buffet, entryway, and mantel. Select candles that complement these elements. They should be either short, such as votives or pillars, or tall enough so that the flame remains above eye level when guests are seated at the table.

Setting the Thanksgiving Table

Measure your table to determine whether it will work for the number of diners, and add or remove leaves or extensions as needed. A comfortable table setting, especially a formal one with a variety of glassware and flatware, should allow about two feet (60 cm) of space between the center of one plate and the center of the next. A week or so before the holiday, set out all of the dishes, glassware, and silver you will be using, so you can take stock and replace any missing pieces. At this time, you might want to try out a complete place setting on a corner of the tablecloth to get a sense of the total effect.

The Informal Table

For a casual Thanksgiving dinner or a meal served over the holiday weekend, consider setting the table without a cloth, especially if it has an attractive wood or glass surface. Or, select a simple cotton tablecloth or place mats in a neutral color and complementary napkins with a similar look and feel. A long runner, laid over the bare tabletop or the tablecloth, in a similar or complementary fabric, is an easy way to dress up a casual dining surface.

You can use everyday plates, flatware, and glassware, adding a few special

Informal table setting: Everyday flatware, a neutral-toned plate, and an all-purpose glass for water or wine. Place mats can stand in for a tablecloth.

Formal table setting: Special-occasion flatware and an optional charger. Glasses for wine and water are arranged at an angle above the knife.

COOKING TIPS FOR THANKSGIVING

- Start with a fresh free-range turkey or thaw a frozen turkey in the refrigerator for 3 to 4 days, depending on its size.

- You can make turkey stock a day or two ahead of the holiday; you can also make gravy at that time, and store it in the refrigerator. If you do, make the gravy thicker than usual, then warm it before the meal and thin it with defatted pan juices after the turkey is cooked.

- You can prepare cranberry sauce, relish, or chutney in advance and store tightly covered in the refrigerator. These preparations will keep for up to 2 weeks.

- Stuff the turkey just before you put it in the oven, and remove the stuffing promptly once the bird is cooked. Allowing raw or cooked stuffing to sit inside the turkey at room temperature can cause harmful bacteria to grow.

- If you have extra stuffing, spoon it into a buttered baking dish and bake it next to the turkey during the last 40 minutes of roasting, or until it develops a golden brown crust.

- When the turkey or ham is done, remove it from the oven, tent it loosely with aluminum foil, and let it rest for about 20 minutes before carving. This allows the juices to redistribute evenly, making the meat moister and easier to carve.

- While the turkey or ham rests, reheat and plate the side dishes on serving platters, cover each with aluminum foil, and use the still-warm oven to keep them hot while you carve.

- To smooth out lumpy gravy, beat it with a whisk or an electric mixer; if necessary, strain it through a fine-mesh sieve.

pieces—an heirloom gravy boat, a modern vase, a fanciful platter—to enhance the holiday mood. Set a simply folded or rolled napkin on each plate, or to the left of the plate, with the folded side facing inward. Arrange flatware in the order in which it will be used, starting with the outermost item. Put forks on the left side of the plate, or to the right of the napkin. On the right side of the plate, put the knife, with its blade facing inward, and the soupspoon, if you are serving soup. Set a water glass above the knife and a wineglass to its right.

For an informal Thanksgiving, there is no need to clutter the table with butter plates and knives or dessertspoons or forks. Guests can put bread directly on their dinner plates, and spoons and forks can be brought out along with the dessert.

The Formal Table

A formal table setting can contribute to a truly memorable holiday. It does not require a formal dining room or showy chandelier, however. In this case, formality means gracious yet comfortable elegance, rather than ostentation or stiffness. If you own crystal and china, good silver, and a linen tablecloth and napkins, Thanksgiving is the perfect opportunity to use them.

At a formal table, guests always have a plate in front of them. A charger, or large plate, is set at each place, and the first course is served on a small plate set atop the charger. The charger is replaced with a dinner plate when the main course is served.

To the left of the plate, place the napkin, its fold facing inward, with room for

silverware to its right. You can also put the napkin on the plate, especially if it is attractively folded. Silverware is seldom placed directly on the napkin, as it inhibits a guest's ability to pick it up easily. To the right of the napkin, place the forks in the order in which they will be used, from left to right. Put the knife on the right side of the plate with its blade facing inward, and set the soupspoon to the right of the knife. Put the dessert fork above the plate, parallel to the edge of the table and with its handle pointing to the left; above it, put the dessert-spoon with its handle pointing to the right. If space is tight, you can bring the dessert implements out when the course is served.

Put a bread plate above the forks and lay a butter knife across its upper rim. Arrange glassware in a diagonal line starting above the knife, going up and to the left in order of use from closest to farthest. Set out a wineglass for each type of wine, and, at the upper-left end of the diagonal, a water glass.

The Buffet

Choose a table or sideboard to use for the buffet, and arrange your serving platters on it ahead of time to make sure everything fits. You may wish to opt for a smaller buffet table, which gives a look of abundance, over a large one, which can appear sparse. If space allows, move the table away from the wall so guests have access to both sides. Set the dinner plates at the end where the guests will start, and the napkins and silverware—if they are not set on the dining table—at the other end, so guests won't have to juggle too many items while serving

An example of basic wineglass shapes, left to right: Champagne or sparkling wine flute, white-wine glass, Burgundy glass, Bordeaux glass, Port or dessert-wine glass

themselves. Check to ensure that each dish has its own appropriate serving utensil. In the remaining space, add a few decorative elements, such as candles or an arrangement that ties in with the table centerpiece.

For a large group, display the turkey or ham whole on the buffet as the guests gather, so they can admire it. Then do the carving in the kitchen and return the carved slices to the buffet on a platter. For smaller gatherings, you can stand at the buffet and carve slices to serve to each guest. This makes for a more dramatic presentation and keeps the meat warmer and moister.

Turkey Carving Tips

The holiday turkey is typically carved according to the style of service. Use the traditional method when carving at the table or buffet, and the restaurant method when carving in the kitchen. A well-sharpened knife makes for easier, safer carving.

Traditional method. Set the turkey on the cutting board, breast side up. Remove the wings by pulling them away from the body to find the shoulder joint and cutting through the joint. Discard each wing tip and carve each wing at the elbow joint into two pieces. Remove each whole leg with thigh attached in the same way. Separate each drumstick from the thigh by cutting through the joint. You can serve the drumsticks and thighs whole if the bird is relatively small. If the turkey is large, slice the meat off, cutting parallel to the bone. On each side of the turkey, just above the shoulder and thigh joints, carve a horizontal cut straight through the breast to the bone. Then carve thin slices vertically, cutting straight down to end each slice at the base cut. As you carve the slices, either place them on a platter or serve them directly to the guests.

Restaurant method. Remove and carve the wings, legs, and thighs as directed for the traditional method. Using a long, thin-bladed carving knife, cut out the wishbone. Remove each half breast in a single piece by cutting vertically downward on either side of the breastbone, turning the knife to follow the curve of the ribcage and pulling the meat away from the carcass with a carving fork. Set each breast half on the cutting board and carve it into thin crosswise slices. Fan the breast slices on one side of the platter and arrange the dark meat on the other.

Serving Wine at Thanksgiving

Matching a single wine with all the other flavors that make up a Thanksgiving feast can be challenging. A good solution is to offer both a white and a red. For the white, try a crisp Chardonnay, and for the red, a Pinot Noir or medium-bodied Zinfandel. All of them pair well with most holiday foods.

Ideally, each place setting should include a different glass for each wine served. Classic-shaped wineglasses are best for concentrating the aroma and bringing out the flavor of wines. A tulip-shaped white-wine glass and a larger, similarly shaped red-wine glass are suitable for most wines. Look for lightweight glasses that make a pinging sound when tapped. If limited to a single glass, a large white-wine glass is a versatile choice. For sparkling wines, use tall flutes, which trap bubbles and enhance effervescence. Once guests are seated, fill wineglasses one-third full. Serve sparkling wines well chilled (42°–45°F/6°–7°C) as an aperitif, with the first course, or throughout the meal. Chill whites to 45°–50°F (7°–10°C) and serve reds at cool room temperature.

INDEX

ACKNOWLEDGMENTS

WELDON OWEN wishes to thank the following individuals and organizations for their kind assistance: Desne Ahlers, Heather Belt, Carrie Bradley, Audrey Candau, Ken DellaPenta, Ashley Johnson, Carol Knorpp, Tina and John Mehan, Renée Meyers, Steve Siegelman, Sharon Silva, The Blackwell Files, and Jo Wunderlich.

GEORGE DOLESE would like to thank Elisabet der Nederlanden for her continued loyalty and calming presence, Ansellmo Valte for helping out in the kitchen and advice on wine, and Ver Brugge Meat for quality product and friendly service.

SARA SLAVIN wishes to extend a special thanks to Sue Fisher King and Dandelion, both in San Francisco.

FREE PRESS

A Division of Simon & Schuster, Inc.

1230 Avenue of the Americas

New York, NY 10020

A WELDON OWEN PRODUCTION

Copyright © 2005 Weldon Owen Inc.
and Williams-Sonoma, Inc.

First printed in 2005

Printed in China

Printed by Midas Printing Limited

10 9 8 7 6 5 4 3

Library of Congress Cataloging-in-Publication Data is available.

ISBN-13: 978-0-7432-7850-8

ISBN-10: 0-7432-7850-X

Jacket Images

Front cover: New England Thanksgiving, page 18.
Back cover: Roast Turkey with Pan Gravy, page 30; Autumn Harvest
Centerpiece, page 120; Day-After Lunch, page 96.

THE ENTERTAINING SERIES

Conceived and produced by Weldon Owen Inc.

814 Montgomery Street, San Francisco, CA 94133

Telephone: 415-291-0100 Fax: 415-291-8841

In Collaboration with Williams-Sonoma, Inc.
3250 Van Ness Avenue, San Francisco, CA 94109

WILLIAMS-SONOMA, INC.
Founder & Vice-Chairman: Chuck Williams

WELDON OWEN INC.

Chief Executive Officer: John Owen

President and Chief Operating Officer: Terry Newell

Chief Financial Officer: Christine E. Munson

VP International Sales: Stuart Laurence

Creative Director: Gaye Allen

Publisher: Hannah Rahill

Associate Publisher: Amy Marr

Art Director: Nicky Collings

Designer: Rachel Lopez

Associate Editor: Donita Boles

Editorial Assistant: Juli Vendzules

Production Director: Chris Hemesath

Color Specialist: Teri Bell

Production and Reprint Coordinator: Todd Rechner

Associate Food Stylist: Elisabet der Nederlanden

Photographer's Assistant: Brooke Buchanan

Assistant Prop Stylists: Amy Heine, Shashona Burke